# *Falling* in Love with God

## *Again*

# *Falling* in Love with God *Again*

## Andrew Giambarba

**DPI**
DISCIPLESHIP
PUBLICATIONS
INTERNATIONAL

**Falling in Love with God Again**

© 2002 by Discipleship Publications International
2 Sterling Road, Billerica, Mass. 01862-2595

Printed in the United States of America

1-57782-178-5

*Cover Design: Jennifer Matienzo*
*Interior Design: Tony Bonazzi*

*To the incredible men and women of the South Florida Church of Christ: loving families, single moms, career professionals, campus students and teens, single men and women—and all the disciples of tomorrow:*

> *Who am I that I have the honor and the privilege of leading you in this most noble cause? Your compassion and mercy stun me. Your willingness to follow and sacrifice humbles me. I could name hundreds of you, and God would nod from Heaven saying, "I am so proud of him" or "She is a jewel in my crown." You have given my family and me so many examples to follow since welcoming us back to the United States in 1993. You have such a place in our hearts that we would live and die with you.*

# CONTENTS

God formed us for his pleasure, and so formed us that we, as well as He, can, in divine communion, enjoy the sweet and mysterious mingling of kindred personalities. He meant us to see Him and live with Him and draw our life from His smile.

*—A. W. Tozer*

# FOREWORD

The challenge to keep our first love for God may be the greatest we ever face. Since the command to love God is paramount, then staying in love with our Father is the most important thing we will ever do.

But loving God is more than a duty—it is the supreme joy of life. We must move from duty to desire in our fellowship with our Father. But even if we long to do this, how are we to learn?

Andrew Giambarba is a man who loves God. He loves God passionately, deeply, freely, joyfully and with his whole heart and life. Andrew is the kind of person who inspires others to love God more. He is unique in his insight, righteous in his ways, tender in his compassion, and strong in his integrity. You will find that the words of this good brother will help you take your relationship with your heavenly Father to new heights and to new depths.

Knowing Andrew Giambarba is one of the greatest privileges and joys of my life. I treasure the opportunity to know someone who knows God so well. I always leave his presence refreshed and renewed, and with my passion for God rekindled. As you read this book, which is Andrew's very heart, may you be drawn closer to God, who longs to be our all in all.

*Sam Laing*
*May 2002*

# ACKNOWLEDGMENTS

I have so many people to thank for their contributions to this book!

My family has taught me more about God's love and my need to be like him than any other people in my life. I have learned God's transparency from my wife, Mariana, purity of heart from my son, Felipe, the need to live life as fast as your feet can move you from my daughter, Sofia. Our newborn, Marcela, has taught me that sleep deprivation is a whole different thing in my late thirties than it was in my late twenties—especially when trying to write a book!

I have been blessed with some of the greatest friends a man could ask for. Men like Pedro Garcia, Rob Kosberg and John Porter have helped me see my weaknesses in a climate of love and encouragement that inspires me to change. Your friendships will be the medal I show my children and grandchildren.

I feel the need to express some special thanks to my friend Sam Laing. His friendship during the last three years has been a tremendous support and encouragement, and the Triangle church feels like a second home. We see eye to eye on preaching, passion and words—and so much more. You remind me of these words of John Adams, the "honest Yankee Patriot and second President of the United States":

> Upon the stage of life, while conscience claps, let the world hiss! On the contrary, if conscience disapproves, the loudest applauses of the world are of little value.

# A LIFELONG JOURNEY
# —AND BEYOND

Above everything else, loving God is a journey.

We begin as the Father draws us to himself (John 6:44). Slowly, we watch as he opens the eyes of our hearts to who he is and who we are. As we struggle to overcome our doubts, his love begins to show itself so dependable to us. We sense that we are in the battle of our lives as we dig deeper into his word. We can characterize it as a battle to believe or a battle to obey, but ultimately it is a battle to love.

The highs and lows of the journey teach us so much about our own inadequacies. Our Father "does not change like the shifting shadows" (James 1:17), but we do. Within a day or over the course of a season, our feelings can vary from the heights of wanting to move across the planet as a missionary to the depths of wondering if we will ever *really* change. It is hard for us to be consistent with God because we are so inconsistent in so many other areas of our lives. When we forget that we are on a journey, we place too much emphasis on the particular place we find ourselves in at that particular moment. For a lifelong journey, we need gifts like perseverance, grace and trust, in abundant measures. These are the real "essentials" of the Christian life, and we need to possess them in ever-increasing quantities.

It's okay for journeys to have highs and lows. I know we would like to be red hot every minute of our lives, but there are too many variables that we cannot control for that to happen. So many elements come to bear on our relationship with God—our upbringing, our emotional makeup, our past sinful patterns, our achievements or failures all affect us profoundly. I believe that nothing affects us more than the relationships we are currently in, however. Learning to separate how other people feel about us from how God feels about us may be the challenge of our lives. We must learn to distinguish between the two if we are ever to mature as Christians. As we learn, we will have ups and downs, as everyone on a journey has.

## Glimpsing the End

When you finish this book, you will still be on the same journey. Prayerfully, you will understand more clearly than ever that the journey is one that is lifelong. One day, when the journey ends successfully, as we rest in heaven's splendor, we will be grateful for any effort we made. At the same time, we will grasp perfectly that all the "work" has really been done by our loving God and that he has held on to us, even when we have let go of him.

> Here is a trustworthy saying:
>
> If we died with him,
>   we will also live with him;
> if we endure,
>   we will also reign with him.
> If we disown him,
>   he will also disown us;

> if we are faithless,
>> he will remain faithful,
>> for he cannot disown himself. (2 Timothy 2:11–13)

"If we endure, we will also reign with him"—the single most important fact about the journey is that in order to win, all we have to do is finish.

## Love Versus Duty

So…why love God?

Why not just obey him?

Why not just try to not make waves?

Why not "gut out" the journey, stoically advancing toward heaven?

Why love him too?

Some would quickly answer: "Because we are commanded to!" Those folks do not look past the immediacy of the commandment. Although it is true that we need to love God, it is more important to want to love God—if we would really know him as he is.

We don't love God simply because it is commanded. We love him because he is exactly who we have always wanted to love. What touches you the most about who God is?

- Is it the fact that he never quits, that his love never fails?
- Is it the fact that he is always the light at the end of the tunnel?
- Is it the fact that he is always a refuge?
- Or is it that he will always take you back?
- Is it his constant belief that it can be done—whatever "it" may be?

- Is it that he is the only real fountain of strength in this world?
- Is it the fact that he is a companion—he is who you go to when no one else can meet the need? (Who else could a single parent or widow confide in before retiring for the night?)
- Is it that he will always make sure you know where you stand?
- Is it that he is the champion of truth?
- Or is it that he is the champion of the underdog?
- Is it that he is tender with the weak and brokenhearted?
- Or that he is a hammer to the arrogant and proud?
- Is it that he never makes a mistake in the use of his power?

There are so many reasons to love him. I pray this book will help you to celebrate what you love most and to learn more of the "love-able" qualities of the God that we are privileged enough to call "Father." If, in the course of reading this, you discover new reasons to love him, then both the work put into this book and the time you spent reading it will have been fully worth it. And what is more, we will see each other at the end of the journey.

## Effortless Devotion?

As a young Christian, I naively imagined that my life would someday be characterized by effortless devotion. I was sure that a heart that longed to be with God and loved him passionately was just around the corner for me—if I just heard the right sermon or asked the right spiritual advice. In my idealistic thinking, falling in love with God was something that would be spontaneous and need so little "work." What most enamored me of this concept was that it seemed so "spiritual." I was sure that mature Christianity had to be like this: the older you get, the deeper in love you are with God, and therefore, the less effort the relationship takes.

Well, it has been seventeen years, and I am still waiting for that effortless devotion! I have learned that I am someone who needs constant revival. After seventeen years of sermons, advice, challenges and the like, it is more than obvious that none of the structure provided by the church will produce wholehearted devotion. Instead of this devotion being "effortless," I find that what is most natural is disrespect, dishonor and disregard for God. I have found devotion to be the single most challenging piece of Christianity—certainly more challenging than evangelism or even preaching, for that matter. Without a devoted heart, all other "responsibilities" of the Christian life become flat at best and burdensome at worst.

Our lives are full of contrasts as Christians. We can so easily compare the times when we have done things out of the over-flow of hearts "in love with God" to those times when we have begrudgingly done what is expected. We know that the difference is devotion. When we are deeply in love with God, each "responsibility" is a fragrant offering and gift we lay on the altar.

So, who is this book for, anyway?

It is for anyone who after baptism begins to feel "disappointed." Many feel disillusioned when they witness their first friend leave God and fall away from a relationship with him. We can feel disheartened when one of our new heroes in the faith proves himself or herself human by letting us down. These are times to focus on God and his love all over again.

It is for young Christians who are caught up in other people's expectations for their lives. So often the minds and hearts of young Christians get refocused on worrying about what other people think of them: "Do they think I am growing?" "Am I doing well?" "Am I a leader?" "Do they think I am a good leader?" It is very dangerous to start your walk with God more worried about others' perceptions of you, rather than growing in your own personal love and appreciation for God. And it is potentially very discouraging.

This book is for middle-aged Christians whose lives are characterized more by habit than heart. Remember what Jesus said to the church in Ephesus: "You have forsaken your first love" (Revelation 2:4). If you are still committed, but not still concerned, you need to fall in love with God again. Many of our churches are filled with people who we know will never quit, but we wonder if they will ever be passionate again. They will not be unless they fall back in love with God.

It is also for older Christians who have their own unique struggles. While young disciples can be disillusioned because they can feel like God let them down, older disciples are more likely to be disillusioned because they feel that they have let God down. There are times when we look at the sins we have committed or how much we have let things go flat, and it seems like a really long haul back. If you have ever wondered, "Can God use me again, like he did years ago?"—then you need nothing as much as falling in love with him again.

Ready? Let's start the journey back!

# How Bad It Can Get

In the journey of loving God, there is no safe passage. Even after seventeen years as a disciple, I am still "hard pressed on every side" (2 Corinthians 4:8), and each day holds some real dangers for me. The longer I walk with God, the deeper my conviction grows about how little time it takes to damage my heart. The Bible is full of admonitions to "pay careful attention" and "remember"—I am as prone to straying as I am to forgetting. I am the object of a continual seduction by Satan to undermine my relationship with our Father. The simple fact of the matter is that the Christian life does not get easier as we get older.

## How's It Going?

You may be wondering, "So, how am I doing with God?" Good question. We all need to learn how to evaluate our relationship with God with as much accuracy as possible. Given our human inclination toward self-delusion, there is never a one-hundred-percent, for-sure critique. Yes, "the heart is deceitful above all things" (Jeremiah 17:9), but this does not absolve us of our responsibility for self-examination. In any healthy relationship there needs to be time spent on evaluation. If I do not consistently ask myself the question, "How are God and I doing?" I am liable to quickly get far off track. Then, instead of making some small adjustments to restore the relationship to its height, I am going to need all kinds of extra time and effort to even understand where I am and how I got there.

One of my fears about proposing this is the fact that I personally know many people who use an evaluation process with God that they would never use with a human relationship. Think about what kinds of questions we ask ourselves to find out how we are doing spiritually:

- Am I productive?
- Have I recently had a victory?
- Do I have something inspirational to share?
- How good is my record with regard to a particular sin?
- When was the last time I committed a particularly serious sin?
- How involved am I in the mission?
- How do the people around me feel about me?

These questions run the gamut from innocent to downright arrogant. They betray a purely analytical approach. Where is the *relationship* in these questions? They simply do not take the Father into account. I see a big problem with using questions like these to evaluate how we are doing. None of them takes into account a relationship—all of them are results oriented. A high score is possible in response to these questions, yet this would only serve to fill me with a sense of pride in my own behavior. It would not tell me anything accurate about how I am doing in my relationship with God.

When I evaluate my relationship with my wife and children, the questions I ask are so fundamentally different than the ones just mentioned:

- Do they feel loved?
- Are we connected?
- Have I been sensitive?
- Have I become connected emotionally to anyone instead of them?
- Am I listening?
- Am I honoring my word with them?
- Is my motivation right?
- Will this activity, undertaking or decision help our relationship?
- Can they approach me with concern or correction?
- Do they come to me when they are hurting?
- Do they confide in me?

Similarly, any helpful evaluation of our relationship with God must focus on relationship issues. Focusing only on results can be counterproductive and even harmful.

## When I Drift

After being a disciple for many years, I know that I have had my share of moments when I was unfaithful to and unloving toward God. I am intimately aware of how bad it can get, and it is to my shame that I have such a weak and fickle heart. Here is how bad it gets for me.

### Combative

> My companion attacks his friends;
> > he violates his covenant.
> His speech is smooth as butter,
> > yet war is in his heart;
> his words are more soothing than oil,
> > yet they are drawn swords. (Psalm 55:20–21)

The psalmist speaks of a man who is seething on the inside—undetected and aggressive—yet masks it from everyone but God. When I am not close to God, I am a bitter, selfish and aggressive man on the inside. For me, there is nothing that sounds an alarm in my relationship with God like when I feel emotionally combative toward those with whom I am in a covenant relationship. Obviously, I know I am doing poorly when I feel any aggressiveness toward my wife and children, but what I am really speaking of is when I feel that same burning fuse towards my brothers in Christ.

During the year 2000, I felt like my emotions became engrossed in one crusade after another. First, I had to point out everyone else's shortcomings, and then I had to vent what I felt about decisions that were made without my consent. It seemed that each week brought with it a fresh round of battles inside me. If all the arguments and fights I imagined myself participating in had actually played themselves out, I would have alienated some very dear brothers. In reality my mind was conceiving of adversaries when few actually existed. And, yes, I was having "quiet times" each morning and being fairly responsible with all my "Christian duties." Yet, the presence of so much aggression, the assigning of such negative expectations to so many people, and my willingness—on the inside—to enter into so many wars belied my perceived closeness to God.

## Uncaring

> An oracle is within my heart
>    concerning the sinfulness of the wicked:
> There is no fear of God
>    before his eyes.

For in his own eyes he flatters himself
    too much to detect or hate his sin.
The words of his mouth are wicked and deceitful;
    he has ceased to be wise and to do good.
Even on his bed he plots evil;
    he commits himself to a sinful course
    and does not reject what is wrong. (Psalm 36:1–4)

I remember riding in a car that was being driven too fast by a drunk driver. It was 1979 and I was sixteen years old. My mother had died two years earlier, and my family had splintered into a loose collection of bitter individualists. I had been drinking, too, that evening, but not so much as to be unaware of the incredible danger I was in. I will never forget the sheer terror of that ride, being that young, that unable to control my surroundings and that aware of physical danger. Why remember one event from so many years ago? Because I did something that night that I had never done before: I decided not to care. I literally remember releasing all the control I had—all the worry, all the fear—and closing my eyes, and deciding that I didn't care if I died or not. To me, that moment was more spiritually grave than any other particularly sinful moment since. I look back on that night as the occasion when I allowed my heart to embrace the most tragic response to life: apathy.

If I am to evaluate accurately how am I doing spiritually, I need to give specific attention to how much I care. As a Christian, I have never again been that cavalier about my physical life, but I have made the decision to not care—always a sure sign of my love for God being weak. Not caring has then cleared the path for me to cross the line and sin. The Bible calls this hardening our hearts (Ephesians 4:18), and it always precedes serious sin. It should not amaze us that most of the sins we can commit that bring sensual gratification—lust, pornography, overeating, oversleeping, laziness, anger and the like—are usually given in to only after we have decided not to care. No one "falls into impurity" before first "falling into" selfishness and hardness of heart. Think of the things we can tell ourselves to justify giving in:

- "I deserve this—after all, I have said 'No' so many times."
- "This is for me—look at all I sacrifice for God, the church and the ungrateful."
- "I am tired."
- "I am missing out."
- "I know what I need."

All these statements indicate that I have decided not to care and are warnings that I am about to do something I will regret, hurting my God, myself and those around me.

### Hopeless

> "Why did I not perish at birth,
>> and die as I came from the womb?
> Why were there knees to receive me
>> and breasts that I might be nursed?
> For now I would be lying down in peace;
>> I would be asleep and at rest." (Job 3:11–13)

Hopelessness is godlessness. An accurate barometer of my relationship with God is the amount of hope in my heart. I worry about many older Christians who seem to have lost hope in real change for themselves and others. Can there be anything more miserable than a life full to the brim with appointments,

activities and responsibilities—yet lacking the cool, refreshing
fountain of spiritual hope?

In mid-1999 I was in my hotel room in Los Angeles, preparing to speak at a conference. The e-mail junkie in me was taking one last shot at checking my inbox before heading out to
speak. My effort was rewarded with a new e-mail from my
father. I was expecting something light, along the lines of "enjoy
your trip," and what I got literally made me sit down, speech-
less. He was forwarding me the text of a note he had found
written by my deceased mother. In the twenty-two years since
her death, I believed that I had grasped the body of information
available to me about her life. When you lose a parent at a
young age, you become somewhat of a family sleuth, trying to
assemble an accurate image of who the person you lost really
was. The note my dad sent me was written while she was in the
hospital, dying of cancer. It was in a little spiral notebook, not
unlike one we would use to jot down insights from a special
devotional. It simply said:

> So this is all there was, though they had dreamed of a
> thousand years.

Her desperation and disappointment was overwhelming. I was
as incapable of understanding her grief as I was of bettering it.

Yet, her sentiments are echoed in many people's lives all
over the world—when they lose hope of change. How hopeful
I feel about my current situation and my future is key. If I am
deeply in love with God, then he is whispering to me promise
after promise about my life and my future. If I am walking with
him closely, he is meeting my needs for strength and faith
through his Holy Spirit within me. If I am keeping him close to

my heart, then I am bringing each obstacle to him and waiting in expectation for his response (Psalm 5). I expect to be pleasantly surprised by the one I love—who loves me even more than I could ever love him.

We are navigating extremely dangerous waters on this journey. The potential exists every day to give in to spiritual adultery or apathy. What could hurt our relationship with God more than unfaithfulness or ignoring him? Our relationship with him can be seriously compromised even when the "results" look acceptable.

# 2

# BITTERNESS AND FEAR

Above all else, guard your heart,
for it is the wellspring of life.

Proverbs 4:23

While on the journey of faith, if I lose my heart for God, along
with it I lose my desire to fight. This never happens overnight,
but gradually, over time—smaller bad decisions turn into bigger
ones. A day without prayer turns into an unspiritual week. A
"small" decision to not change the channel during an objection-
able commercial turns into a desire to surf the Internet without
filtering software, which turns into…. A decision to avoid conflict with my spouse turns into a resentment, which turns into
coldness, which turns into….

After long periods of neglect, I choose a set of parameters
for my heart that enable me to exist in the church without making too many waves. My outward behavior is acceptable, but on
the inside I have allowed destructive emotional habits to take
root and thrive. The two most prevalent of these that I see in
my own congregation are bitterness and fear. Although these
two emotional responses differ greatly, they both succeed at
undermining our love for God.

## Bitterness

Bitterness is the result of an uncared-for emotional wound. When we feel offended or we are in fact sinned against, the Bible has a prescription for how we should handle it. If we follow Matthew 18:15–17, we can resolve most issues. However, sometimes we are called on to simply forgive, without being able to resolve the issue because of where the offending party is at spiritually. Not forgiving is akin to allowing a physical cut to become infected. Left alone, it will not go away, but will eventually poison the entire body.

### Now and Then

I am deeply sobered by the frequency with which I hear my brothers and sisters in Christ express their bitterness. In my judgment, this sin, one of the most destructive poisons we can allow in our souls, has become all too prevalent in our fellowship. According to Proverbs 14:10, "Each heart knows its own bitterness." It is certainly a deeply personal issue, and I do not want to minimize the painful experiences others have had. People suffer tremendously in this world. God has created us in such a way that our hearts are easy to wound. I do not want to debate the legitimacy of the complaints that people feel deeply—people *have* experienced pain. Lots of unfair and painful experiences befall us outside the church and even within. However, when we allow those experiences to lead us into bitterness, we pay a high price and become alienated from the only relationship that can bring healing.

Look at the instances of bitterness in the Bible. It becomes so clear, once again, that the Scriptures are timeless and apply to our hearts across the ages.

- In Genesis, Esau wept bitterly when he failed to receive the blessing that he felt was rightfully his (Genesis 27:34).
- The Israelites were embittered by the incredibly harsh and unsympathetic treatment they received from the Egyptians (Exodus 1:14).
- Naomi changed her name to Mara, meaning "bitterness," because she lost her husband and her two sons (the husbands of her daughters-in-law). In her words, "I went away full, but the Lord has brought me back empty" (Ruth 1:21).
- Hannah wept "in bitterness of soul" because of her infertility (1 Samuel 1:10).
- David's own men wanted to stone him because of the bitterness they felt at the loss of their children while they were off fighting for the Lord (1 Samuel 30:6).
- Job felt embittered when he did not understand the discipline of God, the testing he was undergoing (Job 7:11, 10:1).
- Parents can be embittered by their child's moral folly (Proverbs 17:25).
- Life itself becomes bitter when we lose our awe of God (Jeremiah 2:19).
- Missing the grace of God causes a bitter root to grow up that has the contagious potential to "defile many" (Hebrews 12:15).
- Envy becomes bitterness if we harbor it in our hearts (James 3:14).

It would not be too difficult to find modern day instances of the same experiences that generated these examples of bitterness. God's plan rarely follows our script and frequently tests every fiber of our being. How have I responded to unexpected pain or unfair treatment? How easy was it to pass my bitterness on to my wife or close friend? How often did I add up all the sacrifices I have made for God in order to justify my bitterness?

It is difficult to not become bitter when you are barren and watch people with children be abusive to them, not treasuring them as you surely would. It is difficult when you remain unmarried for years and have to listen to all the matchmakers in your family wanting to set you up with someone "perfect" for you—except that he or she is not a Christian. It is difficult when you listen to other "success stories" in the church without experiencing your own. It is difficult when you do not feel close to the people around you, but you hear of others who enjoy best friendships. Or when someone you brought to Christ starts dating the object of your affection. Or when the person you have helped financially comes into an inheritance. And so on....

## Handle with Care

Certainly, I cannot respond with incredulity toward the bitterness I see. In fact, as a leader in the church, I can be directly or indirectly responsible for some of it myself. People must be respected and listened too, especially when they feel hurt. It is disrespectful to do anything less. On many occasions I looked at the bitterness of others as "their problem," when—since they are part of the body of Christ—it belongs to all of us. To listen to others is to learn about people and what affects them. For leaders, to listen is to learn how to lead your church more effectively and how to treat people with the respect they deserve.

Here is the challenge: when the listening has been done, there has to be change. At some point bitterness becomes our own personal disease to cure. For example, people who are injured in an automobile accident must try to unravel the circumstances of the crash (if possible), but they must rapidly take ownership of their infirmities and take on the most active role in their own treatment. Similarly, bitterness will actively oppose any well-intentioned effort to restore our love for God. The emotional fuel that bitterness burns is so powerful and so toxic that it chokes out any and all positive emotions seeking to coexist in the same heart.

In dealing with bitterness, each of us is left with a choice as we face the disappointments, mistreatments and hardships of life—as the common sermon point says, "Either get better or get bitter." We become a channel of curse when we hold on to our bitterness, and a channel of blessing when we let it go by forgiving our brother from our heart (see Matthew 18:35) and through accepting hardship as discipline that can produce a harvest of righteousness (Hebrews 12:7–11).

It is a tribute to Jesus' love and training that the eleven remaining apostles resisted bitterness so well. Had they not been trained in the way of the cross, certainly the emotional and physical weight of it would have embittered them. By his constant explanation, he helped them to avoid the bitterness and instead focus on the privilege of suffering for his name (1 Peter 4:13, 19; Acts 5:41; Philippians 1:29). His words in Matthew 16:21 are indicative of this training:

> From that time on Jesus began to explain to his disciples that he must go to Jerusalem and suffer many things at the hands of the elders, chief priests and teachers of the law, and that he must be killed and on the third day be raised to life.

Don't you imagine that this kind of disclosure was designed to help them to understand not only the price of the cross, but also the submission and acceptance of suffering that he would show them so perfectly? Jesus was interested in his disciples taking up their crosses, but doing so in a way that would mirror his own submissive attitude. If we truly understand that we are to suffer with him, what form do we expect this suffering to take? Should it take a form that would be acceptable to us, one that would allow us to overcome without any real self-denial and cross-bearing? Or are we looking for a Christianity that involves no suffering?

It is important to understand that although bitterness is exposed in the Bible, it is never justified. Paul called the Ephesian disciples to "get rid of all bitterness" (Ephesians 4:31), for bitterness is every bit the vice that anger, rage, slander and the like are. How are we to overcome? We overcome bitterness by forgiving one another (Ephesians 4:32) and by trusting that God is at work in all things for our good (Romans 8:28). This is the only prescription the Bible offers to get rid of bitterness.

Does this sound challenging? There is hope! Look at the encouragement of David:

> Though you have made me see troubles, many and bitter,
>     you will restore my life again;
> from the depths of the earth
>     you will again bring me up.
> You will increase my honor
>     and comfort me once again. (Psalm 71:20–21)

We must make a conscious decision to let go of our own bitterness if we want to give our hearts a chance to fall back in love with God.

## Fear

> That night the LORD appeared to him and said, "I am the
> God of your father Abraham. Do not be afraid, for I am
> with you; I will bless you and will increase the number of
> your descendants for the sake of my servant Abraham."
> (Genesis 26:24)

Is there anything more natural than fear? With good reason
the apostle John writes his loved ones and explains that "perfect love drives out fear" (1 John 4:18). He articulated a senti-
ment we know at our core: Fear greatly affects our ability to
love. Fear often grips us as an unconscious response to something, whereas bitterness is a more deliberate response. I am
grouping them together in this chapter, however, because of the
similarity they share: they both render lifeless our love for God.
When I refer to fear, I am referring to the tormenting nature of
fear and the many ways it accomplishes the destabilization and
destruction of our lives. Fear is, I believe, one of the most powerful and universal tools Satan uses to keep mankind from the
knowledge of God and an experience of God's power and
grace in our lives. Fear takes our eyes off of God and puts them
on our circumstances and insecurities.

### Healthy Fear

There is, of course, fear that is crucial to our survival as
humans, and certainly there is fear that is spiritually healthy.
Gavin de Becker has written two great books about the role that
fear plays in protecting us and equipping us to protect our children.[1] I am not pretending that you or I will ever live without

---

[1]Gavin de Becker, *The Gift of Fear: Survival Signals That Protect Us from Violence*
(Boston: Little, Brown, 1997); *Protecting the Gift: Keeping Children and Teenagers Safe
(and Parents Sane)* (NY: Dial Press, 1999).

fear of any kind in this world. There will be a time when all our fears will be relieved, but in this life, we would need to disconnect too many parts of our brain to ever live in a truly fearless state. What I am addressing with this chapter, however, is not "healthy" fear. I am not talking about the strange feeling you had about the man hanging around the playground which might help you protect your child from something ghastly. In a world full of evil behavior and its effects, the fear that protects us is a good thing.

What I am addressing with this chapter is "unhealthy" fear. I can best describe this as fear that controls us, fear that would cause us to turn away from God's direction. Natural fears of danger and its consequences have been woven into the fabric of our minds and hearts by him to do the very thing that the unhealthy fears so effectively render us incapable of: enjoying the life that he created us for.

### Personal, yet Universal

Fear is something we are utterly aware of. Whereas we can have physical ailments whose symptoms are nebulous and elusive, fear does not behave like one of those. Mystery ailments with their on-again-off-again indicators can mask their presence in our physical bodies and lie undetected for years. Not so with fear. Fear is as present as a low-grade fever. Ready to spike to crippling levels when we find ourselves in certain situations, our fears are something we know as intimately as we know ourselves physically. Our fears and the "knowledge" of how we will respond in certain situations determine so much of our behavior.

You know more about your fears than I do. You know which of your fears are large enough to paralyze you—whether or not they would weigh in as such on the scale of others' fears. A friend of mine who shoulders a vast responsibility told me once, "All our waves are the same height." What he meant was that the fear of the hostage negotiator is no greater than the fear of the waitress. Whether I think your fears are less legitimate than mine is never the issue. Fear that is enough to affect me is fear enough. There is neither hierarchy nor reasonableness to fear. Fear is rarely rational. Some of what intimidates me is not even worth thought or analysis by large sections of the population. However, this is not enough consolation for me to overcome my fears alone.

Jesus has plenty to say about fear, which is common to man. (Emphasis is mine in these verses.)

> He replied, "You of little faith, *why are you so afraid?*" Then he got up and rebuked the winds and the waves, and it was completely calm. (Matthew 8:26)

> But Jesus immediately said to them: "Take courage! It is I. *Don't be afraid.*" (Matthew 14:27)

> But Jesus came and touched them. "Get up," he said. *"Don't be afraid."* (Matthew 17:7)

> Then Jesus said to them, *"Do not be afraid.* Go and tell my brothers to go to Galilee; there they will see me." (Matthew 28:10)

> Ignoring what they said, Jesus told the synagogue ruler, *"Don't be afraid*; just believe." (Mark 5:36)

Then Jesus said to Simon, *"Don't be afraid*; from now on you will catch men." (Luke 5:10)

Hearing this, Jesus said to Jairus, *"Don't be afraid*; just believe, and she will be healed." (Luke 8:50)

*"Don't be afraid*; you are worth more than many sparrows." (Luke 12:7)

*"Do not be afraid*, little flock, for your Father has been pleased to give you the kingdom." (Luke 12:32)

When they had rowed three or three and a half miles, they saw Jesus approaching the boat, walking on the water; and they were terrified. But he said to them, "It is I; *don't be afraid*." (John 6:19–20)

*"Do not be afraid*, O Daughter of Zion;
see, your king is coming,
seated on a donkey's colt." (John 12:15)

"Peace I leave with you; my peace I give you. I do not give to you as the world gives. Do not let your hearts be troubled and *do not be afraid*." (John 14:27)

From start to finish, the Bible is full of admonitions and encouragements to overcome our fears. God clearly understands their destructive nature. He is not so intolerant of their existence as to make us feel guilty for experiencing the fears we do; he simply commands us to deal with them in and through our relationship with him. Only through growing in our faith will we consistently have victory over the fears in our lives.

## Fight Fear Spiritually

Fear is a battle you cannot fight alone. I am not sure we can fight any battles alone; but I know that the battle to overcome

something that can control me is one that I need God's help
with. I need a correct concept of who he is. I need a clear
understanding of his word and the encouragement he has made
available there. I need to ask for his help every time the battle
rages within. Only through my growth in these areas will I be
able to regain the ground that I have lost to fear.

Fear and bitterness share one common characteristic: they
dominate our emotions, stifling our capacity to love God in
return. So much of our anger that becomes bitterness has its
roots in our fears. We need help to untangle these emotions and
free ourselves to love our Father.

# THE HEIGHT

"To the angel of the church in Ephesus write:

These are the words of him who holds the seven stars in his right hand and walks among the seven golden lampstands: I know your deeds, your hard work and your perseverance. I know that you cannot tolerate wicked men, that you have tested those who claim to be apostles but are not, and have found them false. You have persevered and have endured hardships for my name, and have not grown weary.

Yet I hold this against you: You have forsaken your first love. Remember the height from which you have fallen! Repent and do the things you did at first. If you do not repent, I will come to you and remove your lampstand from its place. But you have this in your favor: You hate the practices of the Nicolaitans, which I also hate.

He who has an ear, let him hear what the Spirit says to the churches. To him who overcomes, I will give the right to eat from the tree of life, which is in the paradise of God."

Revelation 2:1–7

It has taken me a long time in my Christian life to really believe that remembering "the height from which you have fallen" is a crucial first step in repentance (Revelation 2:5). I now believe that it is not only a crucial antecedent to repentance, but also the key to restoring a heart full of love and gratitude for God.

## Doing Versus Being

I am programmed to "do." When I sin, my first thought is usually, "I need to do what is right—right now." What I do when I realize I am not where I need to be spiritually is a very telling thing. I tend to be reactionary: if my actions were "bad," then I throw myself into doing what is "good." I have learned that this is a rather shallow response. Without question, I should be concerned with doing what is right—especially upon coming to my senses after having sinned—but not as a substitute for dealing with my heart.

If you are like me, sin brings guilt, shame, disappointment and discouragement. I remember a sermon in which the preacher said that every sin he had ever committed had been "stupid and embarrassing." In other words, there is never a sin that we ultimately feel proud of, nor one about which we don't wonder, "How on earth did I let myself do that?" I firmly believe that Satan tries to win two victories each time he tempts us: the first is to get us to commit the sin and so damage our relationship with God; and the second is to discourage us and damage our faith about our ability to change or to be used by God again. Oftentimes, long after the sting of the committed sin has subsided, I am still burdened by the discouragement of having "allowed myself to do that."

This then begs the question: will right actions alone restore my heart? Will I overcome the sinful guilt *and* the discouragement simply by throwing myself into my Christian obligations?

No, I won't. Look at how Revelation 2:1–7 (above) describes the disciples in Ephesus: they *are* hard-working; they *have* persevered; and they *are* intolerant of evil behavior and hypocrisy. They have *even* endured persecution for Christ and "have not grown weary." Yet they have forsaken their "first love," thus proving that activity is not an accurate indication of a heart for God.

If we respond to sin by "doing what is right" alone, we will probably forfeit a tremendous chance to grow in the grace of God. We cannot draw near to God by activity, but by responding to our relationship with him in the ways he has ordained. He has said that it is important to remember the intimate communion—our "first love"—as the first step in effective repentance (Revelation 2:4). I need to remember and reinforce the healthy image of a close, loving walk with God. Once this is reaffirmed, then everything else will be built upon the right foundation.

In Revelation 2, Jesus obviously wanted the entire Ephesian church to stop—before "doing" anything—and remember where they were *before* they fell. This is not the first time in Scripture that the call to remember has been issued. When God found in Jeremiah a faithful and tough prophet, he gave him a message very similar to the one Jesus gave to the church in Ephesus.

> The word of the LORD came to me: "Go and proclaim in the hearing of Jerusalem:
>
> "'I remember the devotion of your youth,
>      how as a bride you loved me
> and followed me through the desert,
>      through a land not sown.

> Israel was holy to the LORD,
>    the firstfruits of his harvest;
> all who devoured her were held guilty,
>    and disaster overtook them,'"
>       declares the LORD." (Jeremiah 2:1–3)

The Israelites were every bit as fickle as by nature we are today. In calling them to repentance, Jeremiah first calls them to remember. As only divine inspiration could paint, Jeremiah presents three verbal canvasses to the people, three scenes they would remember: being a devoted bride, being a faithful follower and being holy and set apart for God.

## The Devoted Bride

The words "forsaking all others" are never easier to say than on your wedding day. I felt that my new wedding ring was a most important possession. It embodied a statement that I was making loud and clear: "I belong to Mariana, only Mariana, and forever, Mariana." God has allowed me to honor that vow for the last thirteen years.

I felt the same way about God when I said "Jesus is Lord" and was baptized on January 9, 1985. My relationship with him was my most important possession. I made the statement loud and clear with such passion: "I belong to Christ, only Christ and forever Christ." God has sustained me in my relationship with him and allowed me to honor that vow since then.

But I have been less faithful to God than I have been to my wife. At times I have drifted into spiritual insensitivity and rebellion. At other times I have tried to blur the lines between myself and the world, trying to fit in and fit Jesus into a world he only wanted to live in to save. There have been days, weeks, even months that only in retrospect and with the spiritual help of friends could I see how unfaithful I had become. I am not talking about little daily slip-ups; I am talking about long spells of dryness, deep doubts and insecurities, and wanton and reckless behavior.

I learned that the way back from these wanderings is not found in activity, but in pulling out the scrapbook and remembering my spiritual wedding day. Where was my heart on that day? How singular and exclusive was my love for God back then? How vehemently would I have reacted toward anything that dared to come between my God and me? As I remember those days, I can feel my heart soften. I can feel God's Spirit helping me to remember, helping me to reset my values and helping to inspire me that the journey back is not as impossible as I had let Satan tell me it was.

## The Faithful Follower

If there was one thing that characterized my early Christian life—and that of so many I know—it was an utter conviction that "God will take care of me." There was no other rationale for so many of us allowing ourselves to be jettisoned out of the United States to preach the gospel in foreign lands that were challenging at best and dangerous at worst. I am sure that the culture of the church in the late '80s added fuel to the fire as we were all consumed with going somewhere, anywhere! It is more than nostalgia I feel when I think back to those days. I feel so grateful to have been in a place and time where the climate of faith was so palpable. Unfortunately for most all of us, the climate has changed in recent years.

I have a ten-year-old, a five-year-old and a newborn. The two oldest love me very much and are very trusting of me as their father. They know I am human, and they are aware of this more often than I would like, but they still trust me. How would I feel if their trust diminished every year as they got older? What would it feel like if their secondary environments (school, friends, the community in which we live) started to alter their trust in me? How would I feel if they touted this newfound wariness about me as "maturity" and something to be cultivated? It would break my heart.

The "height" that Jesus refers to in Revelation 2 is the height of love, which "drives out fear" (1 John 4:18) and produces trust. At her height, Israel did not even have to see the plants to know she would be fed or see the stream to know she would drink. She followed God "through the desert, through a land not sown" (Jeremiah 2:2). Once she allowed her fears to rule, she stopped trusting and believing, and she started asking for proof that she would be alright. Her voice in the desert becomes one of countless negative expectations. She is sure she will starve. She is sure she will be abandoned. She even starts to wax nostalgic about the "benefits" of slavery. Talk like that is from the depths, not the heights.

Do you remember when God's promise to "be with you always" was more than enough?

## Holy and Wholehearted

Israel was holy to the Lord because he himself was holy. By entering into a covenant relationship, Israel's part of the agreement was to be like her God. Israel was to be holy to the Lord because he had fixed his eyes on her, reached down to her, rescued her, cleansed her, restored her, blessed her and trained her. Israel was to be holy to the Lord because he had shown her such grace, compassion and mercy—there was nothing unique about her that obligated God to choose her—this was simply the richest of gifts.

On a practical level, though, it is hard to be holy for an invisible God. If I sin against a person, I usually get to see rather quickly how my sin affects him or her. If I am unholy, sometimes all I have is the internal witness of the Holy Spirit whose grieving affects my conscience and warns me of judgment. If I have slipped from the height, it is a safe bet that the first facet of my spiritual life to suffer is holiness. Holiness is all about inner truth and inner respect for God. I would call much more attention to myself in the church by not attending a service than I were to if I secretly watch a pornographic movie in a motel room while traveling. Unfortunately, the absence from service is sometimes the last example of a heart that has abandoned holiness. So much damage is done to our hearts in secret silence. God cares about integrity—who we are when no one is looking. This is why our measure of holiness can so adequately explain the true condition of our hearts.

Vindication factors in here too. Part of my motivation for being holy is knowing that God sees, that he remembers and that he will ultimately vindicate me. Do you remember when decisions to be holy were easy because you knew that God could see you and would vindicate you? Do you remember when holiness was a simple issue between you and God, not about "having to be open" or worrying about whom to confess to?

> Commit your way to the LORD;
>     trust in him and he will do this:

He will make your righteousness shine like the dawn,
   the justice of your cause like the noonday sun.
(Psalm 37:5–6)

I know I am back on the heights when I am making decisions about my holiness that no one but God could ever know about. I know that I have slipped to the depths when I am living a Christianity that would only pass the test of those who see my external behavior. Do you remember the tremendous spiritual strength you felt when every day was accompanied by a running dialogue with God? Do you remember what it felt like to relish a chance to make decisions about purity? Do you remember when you were so proud to say to God with your life, "This is for you, Father"? Do you remember when you *knew* that he would bless and vindicate every difficult choice you made which favored him?

This is where I have fallen from at different times. This is the mental image I need to dust off and clear the fog away from. This is the man God created me to be—not perfect, but powerful and clean. I need to remember the times when my life with God was much more private than public, when my joy came from being alone with him. At those times, what I carried into a Bible study or church service was overflow, not something manufactured moments before. I have to remember my expectations from those days; I expected each day to bring inspiration, open doors and miraculous confirmations of his presence in my life. I expected the best from him, from his kingdom and from every other facet of my life. I felt protected and cherished. I gloried in fatigue and felt resilient in the face of persecution—and all because I knew he was watching and taking note.

## The View from the Heights

When I am on the heights, I am close to him and close to heaven. The air is clear on the heights, and the future looks bright and navigable. When I am on the heights, I want to pull people upward to enjoy the mountain top. I know I am helping and edifying from the heights, whereas I am afraid of myself and the damage I can do while in the valley. I want to live on the heights, with reasonable expectations that allow me to be human and weak, but without allowing myself to slip into the valley. There is nothing to discover in the valley—my sinful nature has made me an expert in how dark, confusing and burdensome it can become there. On the heights, I stay in contact with that Christian elixir called "inspiration." It is my own inspiration, given to me by God himself. Other Christians and Sunday sermons can give me an initial push out of the valley, but they can only get me going, not take me to the heights.

Do not go any further in this book until you take sufficient time to remember the heights. Do not let your present Christianity stand as a condemnation of how far you have fallen. Take control of your relationship with God right now. I look at my wedding video as something nostalgic and cute, but I don't ever watch it and say, "Man, that was when I really loved my wife!" How much worse it would be to look back at my early Christian days and think, "That was when I really loved God" or "That was when I really trusted" or "That was when I was really holy." If we decide to change now, in this generation, we will come out of the desert and see the Promised Land ourselves—from the heights.

# REDISCOVERY

Now that same day two of [the disciples] were going to a village called Emmaus, about seven miles from Jerusalem. They were talking with each other about everything that had happened. As they talked and discussed these things with each other, Jesus himself came up and walked along with them; but they were kept from recognizing him.

He asked them, "What are you discussing together as you walk along?"

They stood still, their faces downcast....

He said to them, "How foolish you are, and how slow of heart to believe all that the prophets have spoken! Did not the Christ have to suffer these things and then enter his glory?" And beginning with Moses and all the Prophets, he explained to them what was said in all the Scriptures concerning himself....

When he was at the table with them, he took bread, gave thanks, broke it and began to give it to them. Then their eyes were opened and they recognized him, and he disappeared from their sight. They asked each other, "Were not our hearts burning within us while he talked with us on the road and opened the Scriptures to us?"

Luke 24:13–17, 25–27, 30–32

These men fascinate me because they walked alongside Jesus for so long without recognizing him. They were so deeply entranced in their own disappointment and doubts that they did not respond—even though the Spirit was warming their hearts on the inside! These men had accurate knowledge of the events, they had personal experience of them, and they had even had the resurrection related to them by the women who went first to the tomb. But they were stuck. They were disciples of Christ—at least in name, certainly not in spirit at this hour—but they were controlled by the phrase "we had hoped" (Luke 24:21). Their disappointments had superceded the living hope that was walking beside them.

The answer for them, and the answer for all of us, was rediscovery. They initially believed. They initially followed. Their hearts burned bright. Then something happened and they became deeply discouraged. They lost hope. You can hear it in the sarcasm of their question (to Jesus himself!): "Are you only a visitor to Jerusalem and do not know the things that have happened there in these days?" (Luke 24:18). Their perspective is that of the defeated. Yet, the solution to their doubts and discouragement is walking right beside them—but they must allow themselves to rediscover him.

## An Illustration from Marriage

In a healthy marriage, there should be a constant *rediscovering* of each other and a constant *rejoicing* in who the person beside you is. This is not to say there are not times that are flat or plateaus when things have become too much "business" or you are in a rut. But there is no joy like rediscovery.

How many people have you seen reach a plateau in their relationship? It is almost inevitable, but this is not the point. The point is, what do I do when I feel like I have arrived at that plateau? In our society today, many decide that "we are just not compatible anymore." We hear their justifications all the time: "We have both changed; we're not the same people any more." Many look with longing at a coworker and think, "This is what I really need in a husband (or wife)!" Some become nostalgic, thinking about their old boyfriend or girlfriend from college, wondering what it would have been like "if…." They look around. They look backward. But the answer is right beside them; they just need a rediscovery.

I feel that my wife and I are becoming better friends now than ever before in our twelve years of marriage. We spent great times together this past Christmas vacation discovering new places to go for sushi—just the two of us. We did not do it because we "needed to have a date" or because it is a proven for- mula. We went out because we are rediscovering each other. We have been having the greatest talks in the history of our marriage. We are seeing facets of how we think that we have never seen before, and we are talking about issues and subjects that we had never talked about before. We are connecting on a deeper level than ever before. Do you know what the greatest part about this is? She is already right here beside me. I do not need to look backward or look around—she is already right here.

There is such an intense joy in "rediscovering" each other. Your heart is refreshed by all the great qualities you always knew your spouse had, and in addition, you see new facets and qualities that you had not discovered before. You can't help but fall deeper in love.

## Dashed Hopes

How about with God? I know people who are stuck in the disappointment of "we had hoped."

We had hoped that our children would all become Christians.

We had hoped to become leaders.

We had hoped not to move again.

We had hoped that people would understand our needs.

We had hoped that we would overcome this sin once and for all.

We had hoped that this relationship would be "the one."

We had hoped that our husband or wife would make real changes.

We had hoped that this job would be the answer.

What is happening? Well, as long as I stay in the "I had hoped" attitude, nothing will happen. How can it? Even if Jesus were to come up and walk alongside me (which he does because he is "close to the brokenhearted," Psalm 34:18), I would not see it.

The disciples on the road to Emmaus were saved by the very same thing that can help us. Notice that the abundance of "good news" around them did not have enough effect on their hearts. It was not until the words of Christ started to light a fire in their hearts that they pulled out of the funk they were in. The words of God ignited their hearts, so much so that they referred to it as "burning within us" (Luke 24:32). They rediscovered Christ and so were saved.

## Learning from What's Lacking

This book is about falling in love with God again. The presupposition is that most who read it can reference at least one moment when their hearts had burned bright with love for God. This is the best news yet, because you will be able to get back there—and surpass it. No externals will help you, but I am sure you already know this. In fact, when I was at my worst spiritually, I resented the "good news sharing—everything is awesome" spirit of the people around me. I felt that some of it was fake or that it was all designed just to make me change. Therefore, I sometimes found myself bracing to resist it before services.

In his book *David: A Man of Passion and Destiny*, Charles R. Swindoll shares a brilliant insight. He notes that from 1 Samuel 18 to 1 Samuel 22, God systematically removes everything from David that he could have trusted in.

> David had a position and he lost it. He had a wife and he lost her. He had a wise counselor, and he lost him. He had a friend, and he lost him. He had self-respect, and he lost it.[1]

I believe that God does this to all of us at one point or another—all so we can have nothing left but to *rediscover* him. When we feel that people have let us down or that the church service did not provide enough or that the friend is not available the way he or she used to be, it is not because God's kingdom is tarnished. It is because God is forcing us to go to the only place that can cause our hearts to burn once more: his word.

If your relationships are proving "disappointing," maybe God wants you to rediscover how much he can fulfill your needs. Maybe he wants to listen to you pour out your heart to him. God listened to David's cries, complaints, songs and pleas. So often there is an emotional breakthrough that God wants us to have with him. It is time to rediscover his listening ear.

If you "had hoped for" financial stability and feel that insecurity is consuming your heart and affecting your emotions, maybe God wants you to rediscover the joy you once knew of total dependence on him. Maybe he is calling you to rediscover his sovereignty and his intimate knowledge of every need you have.

If your hope disappeared the day your child made the decision to leave God, then you need to look for Jesus walking beside you. Maybe he wants us to rediscover that just as he rejoices with those who rejoice, he also mourns with those who mourn (Romans 12:15). Jesus himself cries with Lazarus' sisters moments before raising him from the dead. Nothing is dead until it dies in the heart of God—not even Lazarus after four days, not your children, not your dreams.

If you are in the rut of believing that your husband or wife is your problem, maybe God wants you to rediscover his expectations for you. After a long period of pointing things out, maybe the only one left to change is you.

God wants us to rediscover our call to be men and women of integrity, no matter if it is appreciated this side of heaven or not. In his word we will find so many who faced obstacles that dwarf our own and yet stood their ground and refused to give in to their own sinfulness.

In a healthy marriage you are constantly rediscovering your mate. In a healthy relationship with God you are constantly rediscovering God. Do you need your heart to "burn within you" too? Take some time to rediscover—not someone who is beside you—but the God *inside* you!

# THE CHRIST

If I spend week after week using the Bible to study about character issues that my children need to embrace, or looking up issues that I feel unresolved about, or looking at a specific sin and how it is treated in the Bible, sooner or later I am going to feel dead. At times I have allowed myself to become suffocated by this kind of Bible study, and I wake up on some mornings wondering why I feel so lifeless and so little love for God. The answer is easy to deduce once I am back on track: it is because I was not involved with God. I was involved in parenting or issues or my own sinfulness; and I was using the Bible plenty, but more as a reference book than a love letter.

In the next three chapters we will look at God in his three personal manifestations: the Christ, the Father and the Holy Spirit. The goal of this is for you to feel more in love with God. Some people become immediately put off by such a goal. They say, "But I don't have those 'feelings'…" or "I feel weird that I don't 'feel' that." The fact is, our feelings only change when we *realize* something new. In our relationship with God, if we are not realizing new things about God's character and heart, we will stop feeling what would be natural to feel. If we have not had a new insight into Christ's character and love recently, he will stop being our hero. If we relegate the work of the Holy

Spirit to what he *does not do* anymore, it is safe to say we are not going to feel much love and appreciation for him. However, as revelations increase, so do feelings. Hopefully, you will realize some new things even through these chapters.

## Jesus—Their All

Many centuries ago, it was enough to preach about Jesus. No one needed three cute points that rhymed.

> That which was from the beginning, which we have heard, which we have seen with our eyes, which we have looked at and our hands have touched—this we proclaim concerning the Word of life. The life appeared; we have seen it and testify to it, and we proclaim to you the eternal life, which was with the Father and has appeared to us. We proclaim to you what we have seen and heard, so that you also may have fellowship with us. And our fellowship is with the Father and with his Son, Jesus Christ. We write this to make our joy complete. (1 John 1:1–4)

That which was from the beginning.
That which we have heard.
That which we have seen with our eyes.
That which we have looked at and our hands have touched.
This we proclaim.

I want you to do one thing as you read this chapter: compare your love for Christ with what you will read and see in the Word.

For the writers of the New Testament and their peers, Jesus was their passion, their message, their inspiration. Their greatest memories, the greatest moments and experiences in their lives revolved around Christ, the man. They had hundreds of personal memories of things that they had observed in him. Like any admiring friend or loving parent, we are fascinated by those we love. He was a craftsman whose work made giddy the admiring soul. He was their hero and they hung on his every word. They knew long before the temple guards said it: "No one ever spoke the way this man does!" (John 7:46).

Christ was not their vehicle to happiness or contentment—Christ *was* their happiness. Christ was not the customer service window—he was who they longed to become. Christ was not the one to solve their problems—Christ was their peace. Christ was what they wanted to experience in life. The more closely they could replicate his life, the more satisfied they were.

If they could suffer as he did, this was the highest of honors. Look at how the disciples responded to severe beating on account of their faith in Christ:

> His speech persuaded them. They called the apostles in and had them flogged. Then they ordered them not to speak in the name of Jesus, and let them go.
>
> The apostles left the Sanhedrin, rejoicing because they had been counted worthy of suffering disgrace for the Name. Day after day, in the temple courts and from house to house, they never stopped teaching and proclaiming the good news that Jesus is the Christ. (Acts 5:40–42)

They were willing to look at life, and even their own challenges, through the optic of Christ. Their relationship was primarily with the Christ who had taught them and inspired them—not with a church. They were so clearly committed to *experiencing* Christ. Church to them was a context in which they could live and communally share this deeply personal and satisfying experience of living as Christ did.

If they could be poured out as he was, if they could feel the emptiness of having given all, they gladly did:

> Paul had decided to sail past Ephesus to avoid spending time in the province of Asia, for he was in a hurry to reach Jerusalem, if possible, by the day of Pentecost.
>
> From Miletus, Paul sent to Ephesus for the elders of the church. When they arrived, he said to them: "You know how I lived the whole time I was with you, from the first day I came into the province of Asia. I served the Lord with great humility and with tears, although I was severely tested by the plots of the Jews. You know that I have not hesitated to preach anything that would be helpful to you but have taught you publicly and from house to house. I have declared to both Jews and Greeks that they must turn to God in repentance and have faith in our Lord Jesus.
>
> "And now, compelled by the Spirit, I am going to Jerusalem, not knowing what will happen to me there. I only know that in every city the Holy Spirit warns me that prison and hardships are facing me. However, I consider my life worth nothing to me, if only I may finish the race and complete the task the Lord Jesus has given me— the task of testifying to the gospel of God's grace." (Acts 20:16–24)

They did not chafe at the cost of following Christ because each cost was a chance to grow. They had already considered their own lives over—when they died to gain Christ. I have always found it so unsatisfying as a Christian when I try to take back my life. When Christ is not being exalted in my life, I find it interesting that I re-count the cost almost daily, but I usually refuse to die. When my goal is other than becoming like him, I become obsessed with the cost instead of inspired to count my own life worth nothing.

## 'The Anointed One'

The New Testament Christians were honored to serve Christ, to subjugate themselves to him and become servants of the message. Their message was "Jesus is the Christ" (Greek), or "the Messiah" (Hebrew), meaning "the Anointed One."

Last year, I found myself preaching "directional" sermons many times and messages about the Christ fewer and fewer times. It is shameful to admit, but I found myself on occasion determining the direction I felt the church needed to go and then preparing a message by cutting and pasting Scriptures that would fit that direction. I was missing out on the chance to lift up Christ and to trust that the Christ-filled heart will keep in step with where his Spirit is leading us all. When I look at the messages in the book of Acts, Christ was lifted high. (The emphasis is mine.)

> Day after day, in the temple courts and from house to house, they never stopped teaching and proclaiming the good news that Jesus is *the Christ*. (Acts 5:42)

> Philip went down to a city in Samaria and proclaimed *the Christ* there. (Acts 8:5)

> Yet Saul grew more and more powerful and baffled the Jews living in Damascus by proving that Jesus is *the Christ*. (Acts 9:22)

> When they had passed through Amphipolis and Apollonia, they came to Thessalonica, where there was a Jewish synagogue. As his custom was, Paul went into

the synagogue, and on three Sabbath days he reasoned with them from the Scriptures, explaining and proving that *the Christ* had to suffer and rise from the dead. "This Jesus I am proclaiming to you is *the Christ*," he said. (Acts 17:1–3)

After this, Paul left Athens and went to Corinth. There he met a Jew named Aquila, a native of Pontus, who had recently come from Italy with his wife Priscilla, because Claudius had ordered all the Jews to leave Rome. Paul went to see them, and because he was a tentmaker as they were, he stayed and worked with them. Every Sabbath he reasoned in the synagogue, trying to persuade Jews and Greeks.

When Silas and Timothy came from Macedonia, Paul devoted himself exclusively to preaching, testifying to the Jews that Jesus was *the Christ*. (Acts 18:1–5)

When they preached about the Christ, it was more than a message that began in Bethlehem with the virgin birth and ended at the ascension. God's Christ was not confined to merely thirty-three years. The Christ was prior to all things:

For by him all things were created: things in heaven and on earth, visible and invisible, whether thrones or powers or rulers or authorities; all things were created by him and for him. He is before all things, and in him all things hold together. And he is the head of the body, the church; he is the beginning and the firstborn from among the dead, so that in everything he might have the supremacy. For God was pleased to have all his fullness dwell in him, and through him to reconcile to himself all things, whether things on earth or things in heaven, by making peace through his blood, shed on the cross. (Colossians 1:16–20)

Couldn't you just spend all week simply meditating on the phrase "God was pleased to have all his fullness dwell in him"?

Before his arrival, there was such a tremendous amount of expectation about the Christ. He had been prophesied about for generations. Imagine the electricity in the air when John the Baptist said, "Look, the Lamb of God, who takes away the sin of the world!" (John 1:29). Can you imagine what those first disciples felt when they realized they were following the very man their great-grandfathers and grandfathers and fathers had all talked about coming "one day"?

He himself taught that he was the Lamb, the Gate, the Bread of Life, the Morning Star. He was the one who would save them from Roman Rule—but not as they thought he would. He was the one who would restore the lost grandeur of Israel, and he was the one who would vindicate their suffering. What is my expectation for Christ today? Is he only the one who exists to bless me? Has he lost his grandeur?

## For Us—Now

Christ is still the only one who can save. Christ is still the only one who can restore. Christ is still the only one who can and will vindicate. The Christ lives on, and he is the head of the church, his body. He is the Messiah of history—nothing man has invented has or can ever save us.

The Christ still lives. The story did not end in the first century. Christ lives on in heaven and is *extremely* active and passionate at this very hour on behalf of his spiritual brothers and sisters. He is the Christ who still lives to intercede and be the advocate before the Father who defeats our accuser—day and night. Too many Christians are oblivious to the current ministry of Christ:

> And we know that in all things God works for the good
> of those who love him, who have been called according
> to his purpose. For those God foreknew he also predes-
> tined to be conformed to the likeness of his Son, that he
> might be the firstborn among many brothers. And those
> he predestined, he also called; those he called, he also
> justified; those he justified, he also glorified.
>
> What, then, shall we say in response to this? If God is
> for us, who can be against us? He who did not spare his
> own Son, but gave him up for us all—how will he not
> also, along with him, graciously give us all things? Who
> will bring any charge against those whom God has cho-
> sen? It is God who justifies. Who is he that condemns?
> Christ Jesus, who died—more than that, who was raised
> to life—is at the right hand of God and is also interceding
> for us. (Romans 8:28–34)

Don't you dare read verse 34 as though it had a colon in it! I have literally heard people read that verse as though the rhetorical question is answered this way: "Who is he that condemns: Christ him-self!" No, no, no—it is a rhetorical question, in keeping with all the other rhetorical questions in the chapter: "Who can be against us?" The answer is, *No one!* Or at least, *Who cares?* "Who will bring any charge against us?" *No one!* Or at least, *Who cares?* "Who is he that condemns?" *No one!* Or at least, *Who cares?* If Christ is for us, it doesn't really matter who is against us, or who charges us, or who condemns us. If Christ is for us, *who cares* who opposes us?

Christ is emphatically not the one who condemns. Consider the first verse in Romans chapter 8: "Therefore, there is now no con-demnation for those who are in Christ Jesus." Christ is the one who is currently at the right hand of God, interceding on our behalf.

The book of Hebrews contains another reference to Christ's present ministry:

> Because of this oath, Jesus has become the guarantee of a better covenant.
>
> Now there have been many of those priests, since death prevented them from continuing in office; but because Jesus lives forever, he has a permanent priesthood. Therefore he is able to save completely those who come to God through him, because he always lives to intercede for them. (Hebrews 7:22–25)

Can you imagine how much strength is available from Christ interceding for us? In the Spanish translation of the Bible, the Scripture says that he is literally "begging God for us" (from Hebrews 7:25, *Dios Habla Hoy*). If I see him begging God to give me strength, to lead me with his Spirit, to forgive me, to empower me, to draw me near…how can I not fall back in love with him?

## Together Forever

There is only one thing better than having the Christ live to intercede for us while we live—to live with him in heaven forever. Being with Christ will be better than all the treasures of the earth. We are unable to even remotely comprehend how amazing it will be:

> "No eye has seen,
>   no ear has heard,
> no mind has conceived
>   what God has prepared for those who love him."
> (1 Corinthians 2:9)

I recently ran an eight-kilometer race with one of the disciples in our teen ministry. Surely I was insane to run a road race with a seventeen-year-old who runs with his high-school's cross country team—and enjoys it! The experience reminded me of how much I actually love running—because it is so analogous to the Christian life. For example, if I start out too fast, I can die; but the most important thing is finishing. I cannot compare myself to anyone else or I will get thrown off. In order to finish I have to feel inspired. I think about walking every time when I think no one is looking! I also envy the people standing on the sidewalk who are looking at me like I am insane. And then I see the finish line and the endorphins wash over my muscles. When I can vaguely make out the banner in the distance, it seems to literally pull me along. Even better yet, when I hear the sound of familiar voices cheering me on—I would never stop now—I wondered why I did not feel this same resolve during the last five kilometers. I cross the finish line and I feel invigorated and accomplished.

Similarly, heaven is the finish line that should literally pull me along. Even now there are some familiar voices cheering us on—disciples who have died in Christ and have made it to the end of the race. More than that, there are so many who are on their way with us. Some will beat us to the finish—that's fine—it just means more cheering for us when we cross the line.

It will be incredible to see brothers and sisters in heaven. I have this thought that we will look at each other with a "Can you believe we made it?!" kind of face. There will be such relief, such emotion. We will be amazed that we are there, finally.

The only one who will not look at us that way will be Christ. Can you imagine what it will be like to see him face to face? He will look each one of us straight in the eye and say, "I never doubted you; I knew you would make it!" Being with him will be better by far than being down here:

> For to me, to live is Christ and to die is gain. If I am to go on living in the body, this will mean fruitful labor for me. Yet what shall I choose? I do not know! I am torn between the two: *I desire to depart and be with Christ, which is better by far;* but it is more necessary for you that I remain in the body. Convinced of this, I know that I will remain, and I will continue with all of you for your progress and joy in the faith, so that through my being with you again your joy in Christ Jesus will overflow on account of me. (Philippians 1:21–26, emphasis mine)

"The Christ" is mentioned directly or indirectly almost two dozen times in Philippians 1. Paul's heart was full of Christ. What stands out to me here, though, is his true heart's desire to "depart and be with Christ, which is better by far." Better than what, Paul? Better than marriage? Better than children? Better than fruitful ministry? Better than comfort and rest? Better than recognition? Better than everything being tidy and neat and organized? Better than all.

If you want to fall in love with God again, you must fill your heart back up with his Son. Fill your heart back up with the honor and passion for his supremacy that he deserves.

# THE FATHER

We have fallen out of love with a Father who does not fall in and out of love with us. Perhaps to start this chapter we need to reestablish some facts about God.

## The One True God

First, if the Bible is clear about anything, it is that God's love is unconditional. God loves us no matter what. God does not vacillate between loving us and anything else. He is willing to forgive every one of us. There is no one who has ever lived that he was not willing to forgive through his Son:

> In him we have redemption through his blood, the for-giveness of sins, in accordance with the riches of God's grace that he lavished on us with all wisdom and under-standing. (Ephesians 1:7–8)

David, the man after God's own heart (Acts 13:22), was an adulterer who schemed the death of Uriah the Hittite (2 Samuel 11). He was a man who God loved, not because of his awesome potential as leader of the Israelites, but because of an immutable quality of God: God's love. Think of who else received forgiveness in the Bible. Thomas, the doubter, was forgiven by God. Peter, the one who denied the Lord, was forgiven by God. Over and over again in the Scriptures, the only ones who fail to receive forgiveness are the ones who fail to ask for it.

Second, God also always comes through. He is totally faithful to you and me. Even when we are unfaithful, God is incapable of being unfaithful to us, for

> ...if we are faithless,
>     he will remain faithful,
>     for he cannot disown himself. (2 Timothy 2:13)

God is not courted away from us by his attraction to someone else who is more talented or less problematic than we are. As Tozer wrote in *The Knowledge of the Holy:* "Men become unfaithful out of desire, fear, weakness, loss of interest, or because of some strong influence from without. Obviously none of these forces can affect God in any way."[1] Just because I give up on God, does not mean that he gives up on me. Who did God ever give up on? Why is that concept even a temptation in my mind? Even the people whom the apostle Paul "handed over to Satan" were treated this way so as to teach them a lesson (1 Timothy 1:20). (And if you are reading this book, it is a good bet that this scripture does not apply to you!)

Additionally, all power originates in God, and his power is absolute. As King David said,

> "Yours, O LORD, is the greatness and the power
>     and the glory and the majesty and the splendor,
>     for everything in heaven and earth is yours.
> Yours, O LORD, is the kingdom;
>     you are exalted as head over all." (1 Chronicles 29:11)

Simply stated, nothing is impossible for God. Nothing is even difficult. God is not in heaven scratching his head, feeling like he has met his match in *any* situation. He can change *anyone*

[1] A. W. Tozer, *The Knowledge of the Holy* (San Francisco: Harper & Row, 1961), 79.

and *anything*. For example, he can convert your parents. Some are converted in seventeen days, others in seventeen years. He can heal your marriage. He can help your children. Children who have wandered away from the truth, causing their Christian parents incredible pain, can come back—not because they are perfect or have even perfectly aligned themselves with God, but because God is powerful enough to overcome any mistake we have made. A dear friend of mine recently came back to God after some harrowing experiences in the world. He returned to God, not because he or his parents became perfect, but because he finally submitted to God and looked to him for answers. Non-Christian husbands have been converted, some in two years, some in twenty years. Sicknesses have been turned around and some, still in their sicknesses, have learned invaluable lessons. Some he is still teaching lessons to. But it is never an issue of whether or not God has the power. His power is absolute.

Furthermore, God never makes a mistake. God never misjudges. When he gives us something that he knows we can bear up under, he is always right. God's wisdom is infused with his goodness, not with the evil thoughts of a scheming, brilliant, unchallengeable tyrant. His decisions, his answers and his will are representative of the purity of his heart:

> But the wisdom that comes from heaven is first of all pure; then peace-loving, considerate, submissive, full of mercy and good fruit, impartial and sincere. (James 3:17)

Again, I borrow from Tozer:

> Wisdom, among other things, is the ability to devise perfect ends and to achieve those ends by the most perfect means. It

sees the end from the beginning, so that there can be no need to guess or conjecture. Wisdom sees everything in focus, each in proper relation to all, and is thus able to work toward pre-destined goals with flawless precision.[2]

## Our False 'God'

I believe that, at times, I have created a God in my own image, and it is this "god" that I fall in and out of love with. Here are some characteristics of our "god":

- He gets "attitudes" when we misbehave.
- He does not really forgive and sometimes holds a grudge because he "just can't believe" that we could do something like that.
- His power is limited to people's choices and will.
- He is fickle, having no reason to his plan, but arbitrarily choosing to bless or not bless—or even wanting to sting us a little so "we know what it feels like."
- He does not always answer prayers nor always know our hearts as we pray. He is sometimes busy and distracted and we are a sort of frustrating obligation of his.
- He thinks we ask for too much stuff.
- He does not want to "over-bless" us for fear that we will get spoiled.
- He only wants to bless when we have earned it.
- He looks mostly at the results of our performance, not our heart or effort.
- He barely tolerates our presence and does not enjoy being with us except after a "good day."

If this is my "Father," then I am in for a very turbulent relationship with "him." I know many people who, in the deepest recesses of their hearts, believe many of these ideas to be true, at

[2] Tozer, 60.

least on an emotional level. Years ago, I read a book by M. Scott Peck called *The Road Less Traveled.*[3] I found it fascinating because I am a sucker for a good book that can help me with my own fascination with myself—I long to understand why I am the way I am and why I have the predisposition to certain feelings. The point I remember most from the book (I will paraphrase) was the following: a starting point in adulthood is realizing that if you felt that your parents had a hard time loving you, there is a strong possibility that the issue was due to their inability to love, much more than whether you were lovable or not.

I remember the effect of that thought. It opened up in my young Christian mind the *chance* that maybe the encouraging scriptures about the Father were really true. Maybe he did *really* want to have a relationship with me, not based on performance, but based on grace and love! Of course, as I grew spiritually, that "notion" proved true more and more.

## Saturated in the Scriptures

I believe that I must continually establish—or reestablish—the qualities of God that I will accept, regardless of my feelings about them. If I cannot trust my earthly father, then I must learn to trust God. If I cannot trust men (or women), then I must start with God. He has spent so much time and energy trying to convince us of his divine characteristics. We must decide to accept the truth about these traits of his. We must wade through the fog of our experience and accept the truth about God and his character. We cannot love a God who is created in our image.

Here is a classic case in point: How many times have I as a parent witnessed a younger Christian in the church struggle

[3] M. Scott Peck, *The Road Less Traveled* (Kansas City: Andrews McNeel Pub., 2001).

with self-esteem issues because of a dysfunctional family background? What does this observation produce in me? Outrage. Sadness. Zeal to help. How many times have I wanted to sit those disciples down in a chair and get them to believe, really believe, what I think about them—let alone what God himself thinks—instead of the voices from their past? Hundreds, maybe thousands of times.

What is happening to those disciples? They have chosen to follow God, but their lives are not based on a healthy concept of the Father. They are still basing their lives on expectations and perceptions about God that are more worldly than spiritual. We have to learn to base our lives on the promises of God and a healthy image of who God *really* is—not on our warped perception of him.

For example, think of the incredible gifts that God the Father gives: "How great is the love the Father has lavished on us, that we should be called children of God! And that is what we are!" (1 John 3:1). What a privilege that we have been born into a generation that can call God "Father"! What a privilege that he is our Father, not our Master. Do you live like you are under a Father's care or a Master's eye?

> But now, this is what the LORD says--
>     he who created you, O Jacob,
>     he who formed you, O Israel:
> "Fear not, for I have redeemed you;
>     I have summoned you by name; you are mine.
> When you pass through the waters,
>     I will be with you;
> and when you pass through the rivers,
>     they will not sweep over you.

When you walk through the fire,
    you will not be burned;
    the flames will not set you ablaze.
For I am the LORD, your God,
    the Holy One of Israel, your Savior;
I give Egypt for your ransom,
    Cush and Seba in your stead.
Since you are precious and honored in my sight,
    and because I love you,
I will give men in exchange for you,
    and people in exchange for your life." (Isaiah 43:1–4)

How many gifts are listed in this one passage? He has redeemed us. When he thinks of me, he calls me "his." He will accompany me and protect me. He would pay any price for me. I am precious to him. I am honored by him: this is totally amazing! He loves me—he said so.

## The Perception Hurdle

What is the main obstacle for me in accepting God's love? It is my perception of things. My view of how God "should" work, what God "must" think, what "I would do if I were God"—all carry too much weight in my own heart and mind. How many times in this life do I have to learn that I cannot trust my own perception of things? I have been wrong enough times now to relinquish the desire to make my own perception rule.

With God I think we have to make a conscious decision to trust his promises instead of our own perceptions. For example take Sarah, the wife of Abraham. For some reason—perfect in its wisdom—God had Sarah wait twenty-five years between his promise to her and the birth of Isaac. God somehow felt it was worth it to let Sarah go through twenty-five years of "trying" before blessing her with the promised answer of a son. Theoretically, she went through three-hundred months of telling her beloved, "No, not this month." Somehow God had lessons for her during that time. When we look at these things from the Father's perspective and accept that he would do nothing to hurt us eternally, but only to mold us and shape us (as well as mold and shape those who would follow), we understand. When we look solely from *our* perspective, twenty-five years seems like a very long time.

We have created a "god" whom we obligate to work within our perception of time. We get frustrated when a prayer is not answered immediately—especially when we have had an hour-long prayer time. But we must accept God's perspective of time. Yes, "a day is like a thousand years, and a thousand years are like a day" (2 Peter 3:8). I believe that God's framework in which he accomplishes his will is not that of "drive-thru" America. We get discouraged when things do not happen today because I prayed about it today!

Throughout history God has had different men and women stay put in awkward situations for quite some time. For example, God waited until Moses was eighty to use him. The prophets were walking billboards for God's proclivity for waiting. Jeremiah preached outside the walls of Jerusalem for how many years? Jesus' temptation in the desert lasted forty days— good, long retreat for someone who only had little more than a thousand days for his entire ministry.

And what do I do with the great amount of time in my life when I have been a lifeless son? For so many of us now, the challenge is not that we have had a bad day, but that we have had some bad years. So, what do we do to return to God? How do we restore this relationship? Our only hope is to believe in his promises more than we believe in our own perceptions or the "god" we have created in his stead. We need to ask ourselves what promises of God my life is currently based on and if I am striving to rediscover the Father—as he really is.

Something that helped me was to study about the grace of God. I took a six-month period to follow the concept of grace throughout the entire Bible. I dedicated a special Bible just for that study; I highlighted every Scripture on grace in green pen. I then transcribed every Scripture by hand into a special "grace" notebook in which I would also write my thoughts and prayers about them. I read *Transforming Grace* by Jerry Bridges[4] and *What's So Amazing About Grace?* by Philip Yancey.[5] I preached on it, taught on it, and slowly it started to become part of what I *deeply* believe about God. It took effort, but the rewards were so much greater than the effort. I believe that God blessed the study because he wants to make sure that I know him as he really is.

## Revealed by Jesus

What I saw more and more from my grace study was that we know of God the Father first and foremost, through his relationship as Father to the only Son. Their relationship predates any man, even creation itself. It was primarily through the Son that his Fatherhood was demonstrated—a further step in his ever-increasing revelation of himself to his creation. Now that he has shown himself to be the Father, this is how we should see him primarily.

---

[4]Jerry Bridges, *Transforming Grace* (Colorado Springs: NavPress, 1991).
[5]Philip Yancey, *What's So Amazing About Grace?* (Grand Rapids: Zondervan, 1997).

Jesus strove to reveal his Father to this world. In the beginning of his ministry, his goal was clear: "No one has ever seen God, but God the One and Only, who is at the Father's side, has made him known" (John 1:18). As his ministry to his disciples unfolded, he remained dedicated to the revelation:

> Jesus answered, "I am the way and the truth and the life. No one comes to the Father except through me. If you really knew me, you would know my Father as well. From now on, you do know him and have seen him."
> Philip said, "Lord, show us the Father and that will be enough for us."
> Jesus answered: "Don't you know me, Philip, even after I have been among you such a long time? Anyone who has seen me has seen the Father. How can you say, 'Show us the Father'?" (John 14:6–9)

At the end of his ministry, he communicated his satisfaction on the job he had done:

> "Righteous Father, though the world does not know you, I know you, and they know that you have sent me. I have made you known to them, and will continue to make you known in order that the love you have for me may be in them and that I myself may be in them." (John 17:25–26)

The forgiveness provided by Jesus' blood was a means to an end: our restored relationship with the Father. Forgiveness of sins was simply the passage through the veil (see 2 Corinthians 3:13–16). There have been many times when I have viewed forgiveness as the means to comfort, peace, prosperity—becoming too consumed with another journey and again not looking to the Father. Jesus said it so succinctly on the night of the Last Supper:

"Now this is eternal life: that they may know you, the only true God, and Jesus Christ, whom you have sent." (John 17:3)

I could spend the rest of this book talking about the Father. I have not even touched the gifts of acceptance, encouragement and strength. I beg you to take the time to learn what is true about the Father with regard to these qualities in his relationship with you. Your heart will progressively soften as you grasp his true character, once again feeling love for him taking root there.

# 7

# THE HOLY SPIRIT

What role does the Holy Spirit have in helping us fall back in love with God? Perhaps more than any other chapter in this book, I have been personally shattered but then transformed by my study of the Holy Spirit. I have felt God's Spirit pierce my heart, and I pray that a portion of that conviction will make it through these pages to your heart too.

How can I experience deep love for God—love being a fruit of the Holy Spirit and all—if I neglect the person of God who lives within me? If I fail to be conscious of God who lives within me, how stunted then becomes my "relationship" with God in heaven? We may suffer in our Christianity more through our ambivalence and direct neglect of God's Spirit than through any other spiritual malady. How is it that I can miss God's Spirit when the Bible is chock full of references to his activity? It can be nothing other than a direct Satanic scheme to produce in me the ultimate disappointment: self-reliance.

## Holy Spirit Consciousness

The last book I wrote, in 1987, was a primer on missionary church plantings. I dedicated a whole chapter to the work of the Holy Spirit in the book of Acts. My own words now come back to haunt me!

> There is no one who wants the world evangelized more or has taken so active a role throughout history as the Holy Spirit of God. A sweep through the book of Acts shows us the Spirit zealously preparing, coordinating and conquering the first century world.[1]

That was the conclusion I came to by immersing myself in the book of Acts. How much more consciousness of the Holy Spirit will God give us as we look for him throughout the entire Bible?

The Spirit is present at the creation, hovering over the waters. God anoints men with his Spirit, the list being lengthy and hallowed: Othniel, Joshua, Jephthah, Samson, Saul, David, Amasai, Azariah, Jahaziel, Zechariah, Ezekiel, Daniel and Micah. The Spirit came upon these men, and they led their people to great victories or prophesied life-saving messages for God's people. The Spirit is credited with giving David the plans for the temple that he passed down to his son Solomon. The Holy Spirit engendered the child in the womb of Mary and descended upon Jesus at his baptism in the visible form of a dove. The Spirit of God led Jesus into the desert to be tempted and never left his side. Jesus returned from the desert in the power of the Spirit to begin his ministry. The Spirit of God drove out all the demons and did all the healing in Jesus' ministry. The Spirit of God filled Jesus with joy at the return of the disciples from the limited commission. What else could have been produced in his soul when he saw his plan unfolding so well and he saw these brand new disciples filled with conviction, experience and a growing faith? Jesus promised that the Spirit would accompany the disciples, literally speaking for the first disciples when they were persecuted. And so on and so on…. (I have purposely not included the

[1]Andrew Giambarba, *Bent on Conquest* (Boston: Boston Church of Christ, 1987), 13.

scriptural references for these facts so that you will be encouraged to delve into the Bible and find them for yourself!)

In Matthew 12:31–32 Jesus teaches that blasphemy against the Holy Spirit is the one unforgivable sin:

> "And so I tell you, every sin and blasphemy will be forgiven men, but the blasphemy against the Spirit will not be forgiven. Anyone who speaks a word against the Son of Man will be forgiven, but anyone who speaks against the Holy Spirit will not be forgiven, either in this age or in the age to come."

I have read many commentaries on this concept, and all seem to have one common thread. The lack of credit, acknowledgment and reverence for the Holy Spirit constitutes the blasphemy. In that case, I have come much closer to this sin than I had ever imagined.

"Blasphemy" is defined as: "A contemptuous, irreverent or impious act or utterance" (*American Heritage Dictionary*). As I took apart the definition, I saw how close I get. "Contempt" is "disparaging or haughty disdain; scorn." "Irreverent" is "disrespectful." "Impious" is "lacking due respect."

I do not think I have ever purposefully been disparaging or disdainful, but what else does so much silence in giving God's Spirit credit and public acknowledgment communicate? (This chapter is literally bringing me to tears as I write it.) How much strength and help is there for the asking? How blessed am I to know that God's Spirit "remains" with me? Where his Spirit is, there is freedom to grow, wisdom to choose the appropriate path, and strength to endure—if I am first conscious of his presence in my life. For example, look at how Paul gives the Spirit credit for his ministry:

> Therefore I glory in Christ Jesus in my service to God. I will not venture to speak of anything except what Christ has accomplished through me in leading the Gentiles to obey God by what I have said and done—by the power of signs and miracles, *through the power of the Spirit*. So from Jerusalem all the way around to Illyricum, I have fully proclaimed the gospel of Christ. (Romans 15:17–19, emphasis mine)

What else should I be conscious of, regarding the Holy Spirit?

- Romans 2:29—the Spirit's circumcision of my heart
- Romans 5:1–5—God pours his love into my heart via the Holy Spirit
- 1 Corinthians 3:16; Ephesians 2:22—I am God's temple and God's Spirit lives in me
- Galatians 4:6—the Holy Spirit within me cries out to God in the most intimate language: "Abba, Father"
- Ephesians 1:17—the credit for all wisdom and revelation goes to the Spirit
- 1 John 3:24, 4:13—he himself testifies to us that he lives within us

Every spiritual thought we have is the result of the workings of God's Spirit within us. Every confirmation and every embraced truth is a testimony to his presence in our lives. As I become more and more conscious of his presence, I cannot help but warm my heart to the Master who planned such perfect design. How can I not love deeply he who left himself within me for my own good?

## Holy Spirit Designation

> Then the LORD said to Moses, "See, I have chosen
> Bezalel son of Uri, the son of Hur, of the tribe of Judah,
> and I have filled him with the Spirit of God, with skill, abil-
> ity and knowledge in all kinds of crafts—to make artistic
> designs for work in gold, silver and bronze, to cut and set
> stones, to work in wood, and to engage in all kinds of
> craftsmanship. Moreover, I have appointed Oholiab son
> of Ahisamach, of the tribe of Dan, to help him. Also I have
> given skill to all the craftsmen to make everything I have
> commanded you: the Tent of Meeting, the ark of the
> Testimony with the atonement cover on it, and all the
> other furnishings of the tent—the table and its articles,
> the pure gold lampstand and all its accessories, the altar
> of incense, the altar of burnt offering and all its utensils,
> the basin with its stand—and also the woven garments,
> both the sacred garments for Aaron the priest and the
> garments for his sons when they serve as priests, and
> the anointing oil and fragrant incense for the Holy Place.
> They are to make them just as I commanded you."
> (Exodus 31:1–11)

Lest we become overly tempted to feel that the role of the Holy
Spirit is only to help us experientially, God gives us verse after
verse about how his Holy Spirit (remember whose Spirit he is) is
just as involved in accomplishing God's perfect will. In the prepa-
ration for the tabernacle, which was a shadow of the temple, which
was a shadow of heaven, God's Spirit gives Bezalel a manifestation
of his Spirit for the good of the work which God had ordained. To
the unspiritual eye, Bezalel was a magnificent artisan. To God,

Bezalel was simply a vessel for the power of his Spirit. Compare that concept to the 1 Corinthians 12:1–11:

> Now about spiritual gifts, brothers, I do not want you to be ignorant. You know that when you were pagans, somehow or other you were influenced and led astray to mute idols. Therefore I tell you that no one who is speaking by the Spirit of God says, "Jesus be cursed," and no one can say, "Jesus is Lord," except by the Holy Spirit.
>
> There are different kinds of gifts, but the same Spirit. There are different kinds of service, but the same Lord. There are different kinds of working, but the same God works all of them in all men.
>
> *Now to each one the manifestation of the Spirit is given for the common good.* To one there is given through the Spirit the message of wisdom, to another the message of knowledge by means of the same Spirit, to another faith by the same Spirit, to another gifts of healing by that one Spirit, to another miraculous powers, to another prophecy, to another distinguishing between spirits, to another speaking in different kinds of tongues, and to still another the interpretation of tongues. All these are the work of one and the same Spirit, *and he gives them to each one, just as he determines.* (emphasis mine)

Did I pique your interest? Then let me amplify the point. Look at these references:

> "Where can I get meat for all these people? They keep wailing to me, 'Give us meat to eat!' I cannot carry all these people by myself; the burden is too heavy for me. If this is how you are going to treat me, put me to death right now—if I have found favor in your eyes—and do not let me face my own ruin."

> The Lord said to Moses: "Bring me seventy of Israel's elders who are known to you as leaders and officials among the people. Have them come to the Tent of Meeting, that they may stand there with you. I will come down and speak with you there, and I will take of the Spirit that is on you and put the Spirit on them. They will help you carry the burden of the people so that you will not have to carry it alone." (Numbers 11:13–17)

Moses found himself in a bind trying to "manage" the people of God. What was the answer? Nope. "Who" was the answer? Men on whom the Holy Spirit would dwell would be the "answer."

In this same vein we can examine the Servant Christ. Ultimately, the Spirit was given without measure to the one who would lead us into eternity. A look at the Messianic prophecies about Christ—if we are conscious of the Holy Spirit—will reveal the source of Jesus' competence and power. Look at these three from Isaiah, for example:

> A shoot will come up from the stump of Jesse;
>     from his roots a Branch will bear fruit.
> *The Spirit of the LORD will rest on him—*
>     *the Spirit of wisdom and of understanding,*
>     *the Spirit of counsel and of power,*
>     *the Spirit of knowledge and of the fear of the LORD—*
> and he will delight in the fear of the LORD.
> He will not judge by what he sees with his eyes,
>     or decide by what he hears with his ears;
> but with righteousness he will judge the needy,
>     with justice he will give decisions for the poor of the earth.
> He will strike the earth with the rod of his mouth;
>     with the breath of his lips he will slay the wicked.

Righteousness will be his belt
   and faithfulness the sash around his waist. (Isaiah
11:1–5, emphasis mine)

"Here is my servant, whom I uphold,
   my chosen one in whom I delight;
*I will put my Spirit on him*
   and he will bring justice to the nations.
He will not shout or cry out,
   or raise his voice in the streets.
A bruised reed he will not break,
   and a smoldering wick he will not snuff out.
In faithfulness he will bring forth justice;
   he will not falter or be discouraged
till he establishes justice on earth.
   In his law the islands will put their hope." (Isaiah
42:1–4, emphasis mine)

*The Spirit of the Sovereign* LORD *is on me,*
   because the LORD has anointed me
   to preach good news to the poor.
He has sent me to bind up the brokenhearted,
   to proclaim freedom for the captives
   and release from darkness for the prisoners,
to proclaim the year of the LORD's favor
   and the day of vengeance of our God,
to comfort all who mourn,
   and provide for those who grieve in Zion—
to bestow on them a crown of beauty
   instead of ashes,
the oil of gladness
   instead of mourning,

and a garment of praise
    instead of a spirit of despair.
They will be called oaks of righteousness,
    a planting of the LORD
    for the display of his splendor.
(Isaiah 61:1–3, emphasis mine)

Look how intimately connected the Holy Spirit and the Messiah are. When you read through the Gospels, can you see how much Jesus relied on the Spirit to accomplish his work?

What does this have to do with falling in love with God again? My own relationship with God suffered tremendously when I felt like a "failure" in his kingdom. I spent way too much time as a young Christian comparing myself to others who were already mature Christians. I had some other people in my life who felt they needed to constantly remind me, "You are nothing like Frank Kim! He's so 'sharp'!" and "You don't preach like Steve Adkins or Henry Kreite; you went way too long!" In Mexico City as a missionary, I came the closest to leaving God that I had ever or since—all because I felt like I was failing to contribute anything. "God's kingdom would not only be okay without me," I thought, "it would be *better*!" No matter how much I told myself that God loved me, it was hard to feel good without feeling "useful." I wanted so desperately to be used by God and yet was not, that I began to think he must simply think I am "damaged goods." I began to feel that God was saying, "Bring him into the kingdom, but for goodness' sake, don't let him touch anything! He might mess it up." How could I feel deeply in love with God when he seemed to be communicating to me that I was unfit for use in his plan? However, I was terrifically misled in my own thinking.

The Holy Spirit communicates that everyone is useful in the body of Christ (1 Corinthians 12:18). The church is God's design, God's household (Ephesians 2:19). The only proprietary design is his and it does not include a small fraction of the people within: the Holy Spirit has a role for *everyone*. When I feel needed and valued—by God through his Spirit—then I can literally feel my love for him grow. I know my weaknesses, and down deep I believe that I have nothing unique to give. But what I do have is the manifestation of his Holy Spirit that is for the common good. I am Bezalel in my own way, essential to the building up of the body. My "gift" is never undervalued by God. He never looks at me as different (as in *strange*), but only as different (as in *essential*).

## Holy Spirit Experience

If we are to fall in love with God again, it will only be through the work of the Holy Spirit in our lives. God's Spirit lives to be manifested in our lives and to empower our experiences in order to glorify the Father. The Scriptures are full of examples of people who credit God's Spirit with the restoration of their heart and strength.

David knew that he could go nowhere to escape God's Spirit (Psalm 139:7). He credited the Spirit for leading him "on level ground" (Psalm 143:10). Even in the depths of anguish over his sin, the one thing he pleaded to God for was that the Spirit would remain with him (Psalm 51:11). Without the Spirit the road becomes impossible to navigate, and our own strength proves too paltry for the expectations of God.

What does it mean to not experience the Spirit? Here's what the apostle Paul had to say about it to the church in Galatia:

> You foolish Galatians! Who has bewitched you? Before your very eyes Jesus Christ was clearly portrayed as crucified. I would like to learn just one thing from you: Did you receive the Spirit by observing the law, or by believing what you heard? Are you so foolish? After beginning with the Spirit, are you now trying to attain your goal by human effort? Have you suffered so much for nothing—if it really was for nothing? Does God give you his Spirit and work miracles among you because you observe the law, or because you believe what you heard? (Galatians 3:1–5)

Through six different questions, Paul strives to drive home the same point: You are spiritually flailing and falling out of love with God. Instead of deep faith and trust, they were becoming enamored with doing and performing. The result of this change: the emptiness that is unavoidable when people stop cultivating their relationship with Christ through reliance on the Spirit, instead becoming obsessed with their own performance.

The wonderful thing about relying on God's Spirit for strength is that within us, he has no ups and downs! We do, because we alternate between sensitivity and insensitivity to his Spirit's prodding and spiritual direction. When I am tempted to rely on myself and my works to validate myself in my relationship with God, I end up losing the wonderful freedom of simple love for God. When I rely on the Spirit, I feel a constantly deepening love for God because I see him doing things in my life that I know I am incapable of. For example, who else, if not the Spirit of God, can:

- give me a heart of flesh instead of my heart of stone? (Ezekiel 36:24–27)
- speak to my heart and convincingly say, "Do not fear!" (Haggai 2:1–5)
- encourage me to return to God, no matter how much I have strayed? (Isaiah 44:22)

As the angel told the man whom God had named his signet ring: "This is the word of the Lord to Zerubbabel: 'Not by might nor by power, but by my Spirit,' says the Lord Almighty" (Zechariah 4:6).

The encouragement to return is frequently associated with the promised presence of God's Spirit. I think God knows that those who have fallen are deeply convinced of their inability to return without strength greater than their own. If there is one thing I have become an expert in during the last seventeen years, it is my own weakness. At times, I am more of an expert in my weaknesses than I am in the power of God or the certainty of his scriptural promises. In addition to my own weaknesses, I am an expert in the environmental obstacles that aggressively oppose my chances for the life I envision. I can so easily be the Peter who "notices" the wind and the waves (Matthew 8:23–27). No, I can be much worse; I hold a PhD in the wind and the waves!

My only hope is to beg God to allow me to experience the Holy Spirit's power in my life again. No phone call to a Christian friend, no Sunday sermon, no spiritual book can fill me up for victory like the Spirit of God. I was born of water and the Spirit (John 3)—and if I am not careful, both will become the stuff of memories dating back to my baptism. The Holy Spirit longs to help me grow and get stronger all along the journey of my Christian life.

For those who still need convincing, here are some encouraging scriptures.

> "The Spirit gives life; the flesh counts for nothing. The words I have spoken to you are spirit and they are life." (John 6:63)

"The Spirit *gives life.*" He gave me life when I began to study the Word and allowed him to influence my heart. How much more does he now desire to give me life from the inside out?

> "Whoever believes in me, as the Scripture has said, streams of living water will flow from within him." By this he meant the Spirit, whom those who believed in him were later to receive. Up to that time the Spirit had not been given, since Jesus had not yet been glorified. (John 7:38–39)

I am supposed to be experiencing "streams of living water"— moving water, refreshing water—that will cleanse, inspire and invigorate my soul.

## Holy Spirit—Hallelujah!

I am never alone on this journey. I need to look inside at what is being wrought on my behalf: I am being reminded. I have a constant source of strength, wisdom, truth and refreshment. I have prayers and cries that emanate from deep within me, as the Spirit speaks to God with groans and cries. I am to be filled with the Spirit, pray in the Spirit and worship by the Spirit. My justification occurred through the work of the Spirit, my sanctification occurs through the work of the Spirit, and the washing of my rebirth and renewal was done by the Holy Spirit.

God's Spirit shows me, warns me, teaches me and reminds me. He testifies to my heart that the Word is true and powerful. He carried along the men who spoke God's prophecy—overseeing the words and intentions (1 Peter 1:21). God distributes his gifts by the Holy Spirit, and his Spirit's presence in my life is my guarantee of my redemption. Finally, through the Spirit, Christ speaks to the churches and speaks to my heart.

I hope this chapter has helped him speak to your heart and encourage you. His Spirit has never stepped off the path to loving God. He beckons you to walk in step with him all the way to heaven.

> The Spirit and the bride say, "Come!" And let him who hears say, "Come!" Whoever is thirsty, let him come; and whoever wishes, let him take the free gift of the water of life. (Revelation 22:17)

# INTIMATE COMMUNION

"Mom, my neck hurts."

"Well, you've had it in that position all day!"

The family in front of me is about to pass through immigration at Miami International Airport. I am coming home from Caracas, Venezuela. From the looks of their tans and braided hair, they are coming home from a family vacation in the Caribbean. The one with the hurting neck is the youngest of two children, a boy. His thumbs are supernaturally fast-moving as he cranks through level after level of Game Boy something or other. Looking at his sister, I see that she must be about three years his senior, around thirteen. Her eyes are half closed and enough sound is escaping her turbo-bass headphones to let me know that she is listening to the latest CD by the Boy Band du Jour. Mom is on the cell phone, now that she is back in the states and has coverage, checking her messages and alternately grimacing and smiling as they bring news that concerns or pleases. Dad is somewhere—maybe dreading the return to work on Monday, maybe just wondering how his family got so self-absorbed. When it is my turn to cross the yellow line and follow them through immigration, I have to nudge the Nintendo superstar who is literally frozen in place at the counter while his whole family is already downstairs at the baggage carousel. He must be just about to go to level ten.

What will God have to do to reach that family? What theology will be more appealing to those kids than the engrossing elements of pop culture than they currently enjoy? What structure will appeal to Mom who is already so busy with family and kids? What church program will help Dad learn to communicate and connect with his family and take up the spiritual leadership of all four?

Praise God that where theology, structure and programs are powerless, a relationship is able. I could teach them facts about God, help them to add the discipline of a daily quiet time and get them involved in all kinds of activities, but only a relationship with God can moisten a dry soul.

I have felt like each member of that family at different times, even as a Christian. I have let myself become obsessed with recreational "release." I have lost myself plenty of times in my own emotions, fueled by the lyrics of a song or the plot of a movie. Who has not been frazzled by the latest phone call? (On an average day in our home, the phone rings with fifty new calls that demand immediate attention—and our kids are not yet teens!) And I have been that dad on more than one occasion—out there, "somewhere"—wondering how it all got to be this way.

## Staying in Love

I cannot stop this world from spinning, and I have only limited success at reducing the amount of information that comes my way. But I can and must do everything in my power to stay in love with God, to have an intimate relationship with him, as did his Son, Jesus.

> No one has ever seen God, but God the One and Only, who
> is at the Father's side, has made him known. (John 1:18)

In my opinion, this is an unfortunate translation. Whereas the NIV translates the phrase as "who is at the Father's side," it is treated differently in some other translations (added emphasis mine):

> No man hath seen God at any time; the only begotten Son, *which is in the bosom of the Father,* he hath declared him. (KJV)

> No man has seen God at any time; the only begotten God, *who is in the bosom of the Father,* He has explained Him. (NASB)

> No one has ever seen God. It is God the only Son, *who is close to the Father's heart,* who has made him known. (NRS)

> No man has seen God at any time; the only Son, *who is on the breast of the Father,* he has made clear what God is. (BBE)

> Yet the divine and only Son, *who lives in the closest intimacy with the Father,* has made him known. (Phillips)

> "This one-of-a-kind God-Expression,
>   *who exists at the very heart of the Father,*
>   has made him plain as day." (The Message)

> "No one has ever seen God; the One and Only Son, *who is God and who lives in intimate communion with the Father,* is who has made him known to us." (translated from the Spanish version Dios Habla Hoy)

Somehow, I don't think the phrase "who is at the Father's side" communicates the richness of the idea that the Holy Spirit wanted John to share. I believe this passage was written to give us a touchstone, a template or an image of what kind of relationship God wants us to experience. I believe he wants his children to live in "intimate communion" with him.

## Intimacy

I am not sure how it happened, but somehow the word "intimacy" became equated with sex. Perhaps our culture is so devoid of depth that the options in relationships have narrowed into only two: superficial or sexual. If this is the case, then we immediately shut down any chance of this word helping us in our relationship with God—which would be a crime, because according to the *American Heritage Dictionary,* my personal favorite, there are five definitions for the word "intimate" before any reference to sex is mentioned. Here they are:

1. marked by close acquaintance, association or familiarity.
2. relating to or indicative of one's deepest nature
3. essential; innermost
4. marked by informality and privacy
5. very personal; private

Dictionary definitions are not always a safe guide to understanding Biblical truths, but in this case, if we take these in conjunction with the scripture in John 1:18, we will start to get an accurate sense of the kind of relationship God wants us to have with him.

Our relationship with God must be intimate. We must strive to become familiar with each other, close acquaintances who relate to each other's deepest and innermost natures. Our relationship with God must be marked by both informality and privacy as we share together on the most personal level.

Notice how I did not write in "our time with God" or our "quiet times." Those titles look great on a weekly schedule or scribbled into our daily planner, but what God wants is intimacy, not appointments. While writing this chapter, I thought about three of my closest friends, who are between the ages of forty-six and sixty-five. When I compared our friendships to the first five definitions above, they all proved to be "intimate." What is more, these people all allow me to be at my most un-self-conscious and unrehearsed. When I think of their friendships, each is like resting on a comfortable sofa. There is nothing formal or uncomfortable between us.

Theology, structure and programs can never provide intimacy; only a relationship, in which we have decided to let our guard down and be who we are on the deepest level that we are in touch with, can become intimate. In my own life, I have seen my intimacy with God disappear long before the daily discipline did. Structurally, my life has changed very little in the last few years, but this is no guarantee that my relationship with God has remained intimate.

## Communion

In my mind, words paint pictures. The word "communion" engenders an image of a big wooden table, plenty of food and people who do not want to go anywhere for a long time. I don't think I have been overly influenced by Dali or any of the other painters who tried to represent the Lord's Supper on canvas. I think that my image of this comes as much from the Sunday dinner table of dear friends of ours in Buenos Aires as anywhere else. During the years when I lived in Argentina, I had dinner at my friend's parents' home many times. On any given Sunday afternoon there were at least thirty people who would eat at that series of tables that were pushed together to form one long one that seemed to go on forever. I would say that the average time allotted for the meal, from *picada* to *postre* (appetizers to dessert), was a good three hours or so. We would eat; we would talk about soccer, music and politics; and we would offer our suggestions on how to fix the problems of the world. In other words, we would "commune." When I think of Biblical "communing" I think of some classic meals:

> And when one of those who were reclining at the table with Him heard this, he said to Him, "Blessed is everyone who shall eat bread in the kingdom of God!" (Luke 14:15, NAS)

> Here a dinner was given in Jesus' honor. Martha served, while Lazarus was among those reclining at the table with him. (John 12:2, NIV)

> When the hour came, Jesus and his apostles reclined at the table. (Luke 22:14, NIV)

> And it came about that when He had reclined at the table with them, He took the bread and blessed it, and breaking it, He began giving it to them. (Luke 24:30, NAS)

> Peter, turning around, saw the disciple whom Jesus loved following them; the one who also had leaned back on his breast at the supper, and said, "Lord, who is the one who betrays You?" (John 21:20)

When I look at these scriptures, it becomes clear to me that these men probably had a different standard for "communing" with each other than we do. Even at the Last Supper, John was reclining against Jesus as only the most intimate of friends would.

What does all this have to do with my relationship with God? If I am going to fall in love with God again, it is going to take unadulterated time and a lot of "reclining at the table" with the One I love. My relationship with God must be a feast, not a protein shake or an energy bar. However, if I am reading this chapter anywhere in the First World, the deck is stacked against me. Most likely, my life is go, go, go, from the moment I wake up to have my "quiet time" to the moment I fall unconscious onto my pillow. Most of us have at least three different "mail-boxes" we check during a day, whether home phone, cell phone, e-mail, pager, or that old fashioned thing at the end of the driveway. Some of us have children, two jobs, homework, bills to pay, ministries to be involved in and plenty of relationship demands. Who of us purposefully decides, "I want my heart to harden and grow insensitive toward God"? Even so, through unbalanced priorities and unhealthy expectations, that can often be the outcome.

## Reprioritizing

How do we fall in love with God again and stay there? We must first deal with our priorities. I must prioritize intimacy with God. I must develop a relationship with God in which he knows my every essential thought and feeling. As men, this is a daunting challenge. In their book *Raising Cain: Protecting the Emotional Life of Boys,* Kindlon and Thompson communicate one of those truths we men know to be self-evident:

> In our experience with families, we find that most girls get lots of encouragement from an early age to be emotionally literate—to be reflective and expressive of their own feelings and and to be responsive to the feelings of others. Many boys do

not receive this kind of encouragement, and their emotional illiteracy shows, at a young age, when they act with careless disregard for the feelings of others at home, at school or on the playground.[1]

The good news is that practice really does develop our ability to be open and honest. Some find it easier to write out their deepest thoughts. Others need to wade through the swamp of feelings and filler statements in their prayers ("um," "uh," words like "just" and "Father God" as in: "Father God, uh, I just want to thank you Father God, for, um, just this time to be, Father God, with you and, uh, just want to ask you, Father God, that you could, um, just bless this time, Father God. Uh, Father God, just help me, um, Father God, uh, find out just what I am thinking, Father God"—sound familiar?) in order to find the essence of where their heart is before God. Make sure that you prioritize openness and honesty with God above all the other items that war for your attention. The more we practice this, the more enlarged our ability to express our hearts will become and the more satisfied we will feel in our relationship with God. The emotional eloquence of men in the Bible stands as a high call to us who follow Christ today. The charge from God remains upon our shoulders to lead other hearts in worship and prayer. We have to develop a verbal intimacy with God.

## Retooling Expectations

Immediately following our reprioritization, we must retool our expectations. I wrote this chapter a day after returning from Venezuela. Upon my arrival, the first thing my five-year-old asked me was, "Did you bring me a present from your trip?"

[1]Dan Kindlon, PhD, and Michael Thompson, PhD, *Raising Cain: Protecting the Emotional Life of Boys* (New York: Ballantine Publishing Group, 2000), 5.

Similarly, for years, my expectation in my relationship with God was "immediate blessing." Great amounts of my prayer life were devoted exclusively to garnering the requisite blessings of my environment. I have spent hundreds of hours, maybe even thousands, praying for visitors to church, open people and for my sermons to move people. What is lamentable to me is not the amount of time praying for those items. What I found to have injured my relationship with God was that there was not an equivalent amount of time spent in simple communion with God: learning to praise him, thank him, meditate on his attributes, or simply "be still" in his presence—without any immediate expectations of quantifiable blessings. My time with God was intensely demanding on my part, and when the list of requests ended, so did the prayer. My mind was fully involved, but my heart and soul were engaged to a much lesser extent.

As I have sought to fall in love with God again, it has helped me so much to value the priority God places on being united with his Holy Spirit. A dear friend and fellow soldier has constantly taught me, by word and by example, about this practice. I have learned from him to be quiet in my relationship with God and to try to listen to what the Spirit is saying to me through his word, through his appeal to my heart and through his workings in the world around me. Earlier, while I maintained an expectation of immediate blessing and a fixation on what God would do, according to the boundaries I had given him, I noticed that I was blind to the work of the Holy Spirit—except in those ways that were congruent with what I had been asking for. While I was only asking for visitors to church, I tended to miss or undervalue the fruit of God's Holy Spirit. What was patience when I needed a visitor now? Later on, I would learn that God's answer to my prayer was to give me his gifts, the fruits of his Spirit, which would help me become someone who was being transformed more and more into the image of Jesus. The more like Jesus I become, the more effective I will become with people, and as a result, the essence of my prayer to have an impact on people will indeed be answered.

## As Close As Possible

No amount of activity, production, or level of performance will ever be a substitute for the intimate communion God desires to have with me. He desires a relationship. He could have just given us the book, but he went much further: he sent his Son, and "the Word became flesh and made his dwelling among us" (John 1:14). When John's disciples followed the Lamb of God for the first time, he could have turned and given them a three point sermon. Instead, he invited them to spend time with him, saying, "'Come, and you will see.' So they went and saw where he was staying, and spent that day with him." (John 1:39). For three years, he ate, slept, laughed, cried and "communed" with the Twelve—and with so many more. He drew them to himself with an intimacy that they had never experienced before in a relationship. Prior to his death, he promised them the only thing that could be better than the relationship they had already enjoyed: his Spirit—not alongside them as a friend and rabbi—but within them! (John 16:7). If God had not desired intimate communion, then why would he have set himself inside our very hearts?

The relationship is supreme and central to everything else that comprises our Christianity. It is the "blessed center" of which the old hymn sings and the glorious riches of the mystery Paul pronounced to the Gentiles: "Christ in you, the hope of glory." (Colossians 1:27). With a damaged relationship, the right feelings are impossible, and all the theology, structure and discipline just becomes daily drudgery. A life of intimate communion gives wings to the heart, light to the eyes and strength to the soul.

# 9

# COMMUNICATION

As the deer pants for streams of water,
  so my soul pants for you, O God.
My soul thirsts for God, for the living God.
  When can I go and meet with God?
My soul is downcast within me;
  therefore I will remember you
I say to God my Rock,
  "Why have you forgotten me?
Why must I go about mourning,
  oppressed by the enemy?"
My bones suffer mortal agony
  as my foes taunt me,
saying to me all day long,
  "Where is your God?"
Why are you downcast, O my soul?
  Why so disturbed within me?
Put your hope in God,
  for I will yet praise him,
  my Savior and my God.

Psalm 42:1–2, 6, 9–11

## Deep Calls to Deep

Talking to God is the best way to break the chains that hold our hearts captive. So often, when I am feeling separated from

God, I am tempted to do everything but talk to God. I am tempted to go "recreate," as though having some fun or going for a run is going to restore my relationship with God. Sometimes I just want to go read either my Bible or an inspiring book, which does fill my mind with new and fresh insights, but does not draw me emotionally closer to God—nor does it do anything to resolve the inner conflict I feel. At other times, I allow my schedule to fill up with appointments. This ultimately depresses me, because I know with each successive interaction that I am increasingly less capable of giving all I could, were I closely united with God.

One of my big mistakes over the years has been to assume that I have to get everything "just perfect" before going to God in prayer. I lost a lot of precious time in this pursuit—time I could have spent in deep, spiritually edifying communication— because I errantly assumed that God would not want to listen to me until my heart was "right."

I had to learn that God respects people more than I do and more than I give him credit for. I remember reading Philip Yancey's treatment of this subject in his book *The Bible Jesus Read* and feeling the weight of years fall off my shoulders:

> God has it out with loud complainers like Job, Jeremiah, and Jonah. He engages Abraham and Moses in lengthy arguments— and sometimes lets them win! In his wrestling match with Jacob, God waits until daybreak to inflict the wound; till then Jacob holds his own. Quite obviously, God prefers honest disagreement to dishonest submission. He takes human beings seriously, conducts dialogues with them, includes them in his plans, listens to them.[1]

---

[1] Philip Yancey, *The Bible Jesus Read* (Grand Rapids: Zondervan, 1999), 35.

Once I got married, I started to learn that not everyone thinks about communication the way I do. I remember years worth of keeping my deepest feelings from Mariana, my wife, under the guise of knowing some of them might be "too intense" for her. I felt like Jack Nicholson's character in *A Few Good Men* when she would ask me about all I was feeling. Inside, I felt like saying, "You want the truth? You can't handle the truth!" I was sure she would wilt under the weight of all the issues, needs and weaknesses that I entertained in my mind. After all, as a church leader, I was the end point for all those phone calls about heavy situations and crises, not just here in South Florida, but in many other parts of the US and Latin America. I was sure that if I dumped all the thoughts I had upon her, she would be crushed.

Man, was I wrong.

My chauvinistic arrogance got undone when, one fine day, I let it all go—every thought, situation, unsolved mystery— everything! Mari never batted an eye; she simply smiled and said, "I love knowing what is going on with you." I learned a ton that day. More than anything, I learned that my wife was way more capable than I of handling the plethora of issues, simply because she did not feel the same need that I did to solve them all before discussing them. Here is the extra-humbling part: while discussing them, we solved a whole bunch of them. The lesson lives on. There is so much that I need to bring to God way before I come up with a solution for it—and even before I have the right feelings about it.

Read Psalm 42, partially quoted at the beginning of this chapter. David is in a melancholy fog as his emotions, his longing and the negative comments of his detractors all assail him at once. Half the psalm sounds like he is simply telling himself what he should be thinking and feeling. I love the line in verse 7: "Deep calls to deep." David recognizes that his depth and God's depth desire intimate conversation. What is deepest in him longs to connect with what is deepest in God. He articulates it. And he makes the time for it. He even writes it down for an entire nation and centuries of followers to note—and imitate.

## A Two-Way Street

Communication is a two-way street. At my most selfish, I want God to just listen. It is not long into my waterfall of feelings, however, when I realize I will be empty if I do not correspond by listening to his response. This should be a very simple concept, but the ravages of bad relationships, dysfunctional upbringings and negative self-images all contribute to making it extraordinarily challenging for us all.

Whose voice should I listen to? In my moments of spiritual clarity, I would obviously choose the voice of God. And during the years that I have been following Christ, I have learned to hear his voice above all the others. However, in the beginning of my Christian life, there were so many other voices:

- There was the voice of guilt that reminded me of the people I had hurt before becoming a disciple. I knew that I was forgiven, but being forgiven did not do much to still the voices that haunted me. For example I thought about my previous girlfriends and wondered how God could really have forgiven me, especially since I was sure they had not.
- There was the voice that tried to stop me every time I purposed to do something great for God. It was the voice

that judged my motivation and accused me of doing whatever I was doing for self. Since no one's motivations are one-hundred percent pure all the time, this voice stopped me in my tracks more than once.

- There was the voice that told me that people knew I was uniquely weak. If I locked eyes with a leader in the church, I was sure he or she could see right through to the last evil thought in my heart. "They will never trust you," the voice would say, "because you are different," with "different" meaning worse.

- There was the voice of past failures. This voice could get my heart racing in a second. The instant I received a new responsibility, this voice was first in line to remind me of the people I had hurt, the bad decisions I had made, and all I still needed before I would be "capable."

- There was the voice of parental ambivalence. Never before in my life had I even remembered half the comments I had heard about myself from my family. Now, as I desired to dream about becoming a powerful man of God, the memories came flooding back. The worst one was my own father's voice telling me one day that all I would ever be was average.

Maybe you can relate to some of these, and certainly you have your own list, as well. The question then becomes: who do I listen to?

There is a reason for all these voices. I earned many of them by my own sinful behavior. By the time I became a Christian, the sins of immorality, deceit and drug use had done a good job of wrecking my character. Not only had they alienated me from God, but they had built into my character a deep sense of being someone who was disappointing to himself and others. This is the legacy of sin. It affects in real time, and it has time-release effects, too. Long after the acts have ceased, their emotional toll lingers, like talons deeply embedded in our self-esteem. As for my family's negative comments, I can forgive them because I have seen my own need for grace and forgiveness in the same area. I am now an edifying parent for my kids by the grace of God—not because of any naturally formed goodness in me.

To deal with those other voices, I needed to memorize verses and principles from the Bible that would help me to determine what the truth was. I also had to hone my listening skills in order to pick out God's voice above the din. I learned that he had plenty to say about disciplining my mind so that I could participate more fully in my relationship with him. Here are some examples:

> While they were still talking about this, Jesus himself stood among them and said to them, "Peace be with you."
>
> They were startled and frightened, thinking they saw a ghost. He said to them, "Why are you troubled, and *why do doubts rise in your minds?* Look at my hands and my feet. It is I myself! Touch me and see; a ghost does not have flesh and bones, as you see I have."
>
> When he had said this, he showed them his hands and feet. (Luke 24:36–40, emphasis mine)

> Rather, clothe yourselves with the Lord Jesus Christ, and do not *think about* how to gratify the desires of the sinful nature. (Romans 13:14, emphasis mine)

> Surely you heard of him and were taught in him in accordance with the truth that is in Jesus. You were taught, with regard to your former way of life, to put off your old

> self, which is being corrupted by its deceitful desires; to be made new in the attitude of your minds. (Ephesians 4:21–23)

> Since, then, you have been raised with Christ, set your hearts on things above, where Christ is seated at the right hand of God. Set your minds on things above, not on earthly things. (Colossians 3:1–2)

I asked one of the sector leaders in our church to explain to me what he has done to overcome the voices that held him captive for so long. He uses a type of template to help him identify both his feelings and what God would say to him through his word (see facing table). I have found this to be a very pragmatic way to work at overcoming the voices. (Note: it does take work. No amount of warm, fuzzy thinking will eradicate these voices. They must be fought and defeated over and over again.)

## Affectionate Communication

> "Therefore I [the Lord] am now going to allure her;
>    I will lead her into the desert
>    and speak tenderly to her.
> There I will give her back her vineyards,
>    and will make the Valley of Achor a door of hope.
> There she will sing as in the days of her youth,
>    as in the day she came up out of Egypt.
> "In that day," declares the LORD,
>    "you will call me 'my husband';
>    you will no longer call me 'my master.'" (Hosea 2:14–16)

| Thought/fear | What is the worst thing that can happen? | Truth | Scripture |
|---|---|---|---|
| I'll never change. | I could try and fail. | God can do anything. | *Ephesians 3:20*—"Now to him who is able to do immeasurably more than all we ask or imagine, according to his power that is at work within us." |
| I'm an idiot. | I could look foolish. | We all look stupid sometimes. It won't kill me. | *Psalm 139:14*—"I praise you because I am fearfully and wonderfully made; your works are wonderful, I know that full well." |
| How can I help anybody? | I'll try to help and nothing will change. | God will work. I can only share the Word with them. It's up to them to respond. | *2 Corinthians 5:20*—"We are therefore Christ's ambassadors, as though God were making his appeal through us." |
| I don't feel that God is with me. | I go through a time when I feel disconnected. | God promised that he would never leave me. | *Matthew 28:20*—"And surely I am with you always, to the very end of the age." |
| Why would God let _____ happen to me? | I'll go through a hard time and experience some pain. | God has a great plan for my life. | *Romans 8:28*—"And we know that in all things God works for the good of those who love him, who have been called according to his purpose." |
| You'll never amount to anything great. | My dreams and expectations don't become reality. | God has a dream for me. | *Jeremiah 29:11*—"For I know the plans I have for you," declares the Lord, "plans to prosper you and not to harm you, plans to give you hope and a future." |

God wants to speak tenderly to us. This was the hardest truth of all for me to accept. When I first read the New Testament, I saw Jesus as "the great exposer of hearts." Of course, that was because my heart was being exposed for the first time! God's Spirit was uniquely involved in revealing my heart as part of his work to convict me of my sin. This work never really ends, but there is more to the study of the Scriptures than just convicting me after all.

God's word contains God's voice. He is committed to communicating through his word. He wants us to understand the whole gamut of messages he has for us. Foremost in his word is a message of love. I am sorely tempted to write out a list of all the Scriptures that mean the most to me—but I want to encourage you to find your own. Here's a hint: start in chapter 40 of Isaiah and continue looking through the end of the book—amazing! Then branch out and find some more. God speaks tenderly to his children, especially when we ask to find that facet of his heart in his word.

# 10

# HEAVEN IN HEAVEN

Ah, heaven...the dwelling place of God...our soul's rest... streets of gold...no more tears...and few things motivate us less when we lose our love for God. It feels heretical to even write that statement, but it's the truth! How far have I fallen when heaven no longer gives wings to my heart? What corrosion of the soul has entered through my eyes or ears and tainted this promise of promises? Is there any indicator more stark of how cool my love for the Father has gotten? How I feel about heaven betrays my real feelings toward God.

## An Old Testament Heart for Heaven

Heaven has always been very real to spiritual people. They have been confident that God listens from heaven, that God speaks from heaven. Certainly, those under an inferior covenant to ours—when Israel was God's servant, not God's son—appreciated and revered heaven. The dew and the rain came from heaven; it was a gift and a blessing, not a meteorological event. Bread came from heaven, as did the instructions of God. Men and women were called from heaven. Prayers, cries and even criticisms made it all the way up to heaven and into God's listening ear. When people were humbled, their eyes looked up to heaven and their arms extended out as if to reach up and embrace their King. God heard the humble from heaven: he heard and upheld, he heard and defended, he heard and answered, and he heard and forgave. Those who loved him embarked on their missions and made their sacrifices in the name of the God of heaven. The greatest works were always done by those who understood their proximity to heaven at their appointed hour. For them, heaven was the source of all help, all judgment and constant supervision.

In Old Testament times, heaven was also viewed as the place where every one of God's attributes lived in unadulterated purity. Heaven was the seat of righteousness, incorruptible and blinding in its light. Heaven was the limitless fountain of love; all blessings flowed downward from the Father's throne. Nothing came down from heaven that would not build up, refine, perfect and strengthen—except once. Only once in history was anyone expelled from heaven, and that was because his love for his own throne overtook his love for the King.

No, heaven was never to be trifled with. No one swore by heaven lightly because heaven listened. Words were to be uttered carefully because heaven measured. And heaven judged. Heaven was never to be challenged. King Nebuchadnezzar lost his royal authority, his kingdom and even his mind because he fancied himself a threat to heaven. The prophet made it very clear: "Your kingdom will be restored to you when you acknowledge that Heaven rules" (Daniel 4:26).

Heaven was inhabited—filled to overflowing—unable to contain the God who made his throne there. Heaven was loud, filled with praise and rejoicing over sinners who repented and the implementation of God's righteous acts. Mercy and grace flowed from heaven; in fact it was their only source. Man was incapable of manufacturing what heaven exports: joy, peace, love, purity and most of all, forgiveness. Like every majestically designed piece of creation—from the mountains in their grandeur to the intricacies of worlds the human eye cannot peer into—every creation was conceived of in heaven first. If all the world is a stage, then heaven is the front row balcony with the bird's-eye view of all that occurs on, in and under the earth, as well as in the depths of the human mind and heart.

Heaven was enough. David issues one of the greatest challenges our hearts can receive with his passionate cry: "Whom have I in heaven but you? And earth has nothing I desire besides you" (Psalm 73:25). There was never meant to be a rivalry between heaven and the world "under heaven." Certainly, there was no competition between what this world could offer and what blessings would meet us if God were to "throw open the floodgates of heaven" (Malachi 3:10). Even God's kingdom on this earth would only be, at its best, a shadow of the kingdom of heaven *in* heaven.

## Through Jesus' Eyes

Heaven got even better when Jesus came. He helped us understand something crucial about heaven: our Father lives there. No longer would we look up to heaven and think, "Master," "King" or "Jehovah" *only*. No, the overriding title of sovereignty in heaven under the New Covenant has become "Father." The Spirit within us calls out to heaven even more intimately. "Abba," he cries and *Abba* always hears.

As heaven was mentioned in the Gospels and in the New Testament letters, it was as if it was moving nearer and nearer to mankind. Jesus' message of "the kingdom of heaven" filled minds with urgency and zeal. We were to become like children and be born of water and the Spirit to see and gain access to this kingdom that would be man's clearest glimpse thus far of heaven above. We were to store up treasures for ourselves there, indicating an immediacy that man had never grappled with before.

Heaven took on an interactivity with every new teaching of Jesus. He was from there. He would return there. He would acknowledge—or disown—us before his Father there. When he looked up to heaven, fish were multiplied, eyes and ears were opened, and people received back their dead. He seemed to exist on earth and in heaven in real time. From him we learned that heaven is full of angels: children have angels and churches have angels and some of those angels even come from heaven to enter our reality. Angels might even let us entertain them if we are hospitable. But the most important heavenly inhabitant to Jesus was his Father whom he dearly missed. They had a relationship that obviously began in heaven, and his friends could hear his longing as he spoke about that. He made sure to command that we never referred to anyone here on earth as "Father" because we had one Father—his Father—who waited in heaven.

Jesus' Father spoke to him from heaven. He told everyone who would listen: "You are my Son, whom I love; with you I am well pleased" (Mark 1:11). From heaven, his Father gave him the Holy Spirit in the form of a dove and all the authority of both Heaven and earth. After his death, burial and resurrection, he returned to heaven, ascending right before the eyes of those who loved him. In heaven he wrote our names individually and in his own blood. From heaven he sent us the Holy Spirit to counsel, comfort and guide us into all wisdom. From heaven he is our advocate, begging God on our behalf. From heaven he assures us that he is the first of many brothers and sisters to enter heaven itself if we will but overcome. From heaven he shouts through the Spirit that he is unashamed to be called our brother.

From heaven he directs the spreading of his message. With a violent wind from heaven, he ignited the early church and helped them to be victorious in the face of intense persecution. His was and is the only name under heaven by which men must be saved. From heaven he saluted the martyr Stephen, rising from his throne in a one-of-a-kind show of solidarity for one whose heart and treasure were in the same heavenly place. From heaven he sent a light that blinded Saul and illuminated the heart of Paul with a vision that he would not disobey. From heaven he chastised Peter for doubting that his grace would extend to the Gentiles. And from heaven he sent his Spirit as a guarantee of what was to come.

## Sharper and Sharper Focus

As we get closer to heaven, the fog lifts from our hearts and we can see enough to know it will be unlike anything man could ever conceive of! However, we do have various hints here below. We know that our family on earth derives its name from our family in heaven. We know that every knee will bow—even in heaven itself on the day Christ is revealed. We know that our hope and our citizenship is there, along with an inheritance that can never perish, spoil or fade. We know that his coming from there will be announced with the trumpets of heaven and with blazing fire and with powerful angels, the very armies of heaven. And it will all happen in the blink of an eye....

If we are in love with God, we will be ready. By faith, we know that Jesus is preparing a place for each of us who have followed him:

> "Do not let your hearts be troubled. Trust in God; trust also in me. In my Father's house are many rooms; if it were not so, I would have told you. I am going there to prepare a place for you. And if I go and prepare a place for you, I will come back and take you to be with me that you also may be where I am. You know the way to the place where I am going." (John 14:1–4)

I have heard all the anecdotes about God making little theme parks for people—great fishing for the fishermen, tennis courts for the tennis fans—but I do not have a clue. Yet, it is hard for me to believe that God's idea of heaven is "recreational"; this sounds like twenty-first century America to me. What moves me is that it is personal. The One who created me—who knows my intricacies and heart and *all* my weaknesses—is preparing a place for me. To me, this is not about custom home building but about expectation. He is building a place for me, not as Bob Vila would, but as a friend who literally wants me to be *with* him for eternity. He wants me to know that he wants me there with him.

In the last words of Jesus' final prayer on earth, he expresses his heart again:

> "Father, I want those you have given me to be with me where I am, and to see my glory, the glory you have given

me because you loved me before the creation of the
world." (John 17:24)

On the deepest level, he just longs for us to be with him where
he is. This will only appeal to you if you love Jesus back. Yes,
the goal of my faith is the salvation of my soul. But the salvation of my soul is that I might be with him where he is forever:
he said, "Now this is eternal life: that they may know you, the
only true God, and Jesus Christ, whom you have sent" (John
17:3). If I love him, I want to be with him in heaven desperately. It is not just the peace of heaven that draws me, nor the
promise of no tears, or no trials. These appeal to me, but it must
be more to *be* with him. I must want to rest in the arms of my
Father and recline on the breast of my friend, experiencing no
shame and feeling completely safe—a longing fulfilled.

## Heaven on Earth?

So many times I want heaven on earth.

> It is written: "I believed; therefore I have spoken." With
> that same spirit of faith we also believe and therefore
> speak, because we know that the one who raised the
> Lord Jesus from the dead will also raise us with Jesus
> and present us with you in his presence. All this is for
> your benefit, so that the grace that is reaching more and
> more people may cause thanksgiving to overflow to the
> glory of God.
>
> Therefore we do not lose heart. Though outwardly we
> are wasting away, yet inwardly we are being renewed day
> by day. For our light and momentary troubles are achieving
> for us an eternal glory that far outweighs them all. So we fix
> our eyes not on what is seen, but on what is unseen. For

what is seen is temporary, but what is unseen is eternal.
(2 Corinthians 4:13–18)

If I think about the seven days before I wrote this chapter, I am ashamed by how little time I spent "fixing my eyes on what is unseen." It is completely unnatural, but completely essential. When I focus on what is eternal, I feel refreshed. When I focus on what is seen, I feel unsure, clouded and drained. What is worse, when I stop focusing on heaven in heaven and start to expect heaven on Earth, I am sure to become frustrated, bitter and unsatisfied.

> Now we know that if the earthly tent we live in is destroyed, we have a building from God, an eternal house in heaven, not built by human hands. Meanwhile we groan, longing to be clothed with our heavenly dwelling, because when we are clothed, we will not be found naked. For while we are in this tent, we groan and are burdened, because we do not wish to be unclothed but to be clothed with our heavenly dwelling, so that what is mortal may be swallowed up by life. (2 Corinthians 5:1–4)

When I am not content to wait for heaven in heaven, my groaning is never about spiritual things.

Expectations are funny things. On Earth, they frequently disappoint. The only expectations that exceed our imagination are those which are satisfied from heaven. I have hurt my relationship with God when I have placed expectations on the people around me to help build my little piece of heaven on this earth. And usually, I have compounded the problem by expecting them to be mind-readers at the same time! I have needed to learn the hard way that the Bible does not encourage us to expect heaven on Earth. The scriptural expectation for our lives here includes groaning, struggling and being tested. (On the other hand, God expects our expectations for perfection to be for heaven in heaven.)

> I, John, your brother and companion in the suffering and kingdom and patient endurance that are ours in Jesus, was on the island of Patmos because of the word of God and the testimony of Jesus. (Revelation 1:9)

Too many times I have lost my love for God because I was surprised by suffering. Instead of developing a Biblical perspective on it, I took the easy road of "How can this be happening to me?" I love the juxtaposition of the words in the verse above: "suffering" and "patient endurance" and the kingdom is in the middle. I must maintain a deep conviction that the only place on this earth where there is comfort is in my relationship with God. This flies in the face of the world in which we live. Every signal, every advertisement, every stimulus that enters our hearts through our senses says: "You deserve comfort, *now!*" No wonder I can turn so quickly to blaming God for my circumstances.

I have seen so many Christians in the last few years become obsessed with how they are treated inside and outside of the church. It seems like the number of conflicts among Christians has multiplied. Is it because people are being more sinful in their treatment of each other? I don't think so. I think it is because we have errantly promoted the "perfection" of the kingdom of God to a degree that people expect perfection in everything. Heaven is in heaven. Heaven is not even in the kingdom of God on this earth. Here is how we are to be while here:

> Be completely humble and gentle; be patient, bearing with
> one another in love. Make every effort to keep the unity of
> the Spirit through the bond of peace. (Ephesians 4:2–3)

Or as J. B. Phillips translates it, "Accept life with humility and patience, generously making allowances for each other because you love each other."

## Should I Stay or Should I Go?

As I mentioned in chapter 5, the apostle Paul succinctly expressed the conflict between being on Earth and being in heaven in his letter to the Philippians:

> I am torn between the two: I desire to depart and be with
> Christ, which is better by far; but it is more necessary for
> you that I remain in the body. Convinced of this, I know
> that I will remain, and I will continue with all of you for your
> progress and joy in the faith. (Philippians 1:23–25)

He longed to go, but he stayed so that he and others could grow. I love this passage because he works through the issues in his heart right in front of everyone. He had no delusions about where heaven was.

A wonderful sister shared an insight with me from the following passage that inspired me.

> You are not to do as we do here today, everyone as he
> sees fit, since you have not yet reached the resting place
> and the inheritance the LORD your God is giving you. But

you will cross the Jordan and settle in the land the LORD
your God is giving you as an inheritance, and he will give
you rest from all your enemies around you so that you will
live in safety. (Deuteronomy 12:8–10)

She wrote: "I read this scripture this morning and it reminded
me of heaven. Moses told them not to do whatever they wanted because that was not their resting place. The same happens
with us today; we don't do 'as we see fit' because this is not our
resting place—heaven is. That is our inheritance. Since the
beginning of time, God has always tried to persuade his people
to look above. I love that!"

If I keep looking "above" God will soften my heart and I
will fall in love with him again.

# 11

# PRACTICAL INSPIRATION

This chapter is all about the practical. Much of what you will read here came out of a staff meeting that we had this year in South Florida during which I asked the men and women on the ministry staff what special things they do when they feel their love for God waning. What followed was one of the most inspirational times I have been part of! Each person's sharing was followed by a collective "Amen!" It became clear that there are so many things we can do when we find ourselves feeling dry on the inside. Some ideas were just plain spectacular, and more than one of us made a mental note to implement them soon. The meeting ended with everyone understanding, on a much deeper level, why it is important that we are a body. As with all the other chapters in this book, this one is just a compilation of a whole lot of people's good ideas. I am so thankful to God that we don't have to go it alone or only depend on ourselves for inspiration, but that we can belong to an encouraging body.

I respect these brothers and sisters so much. They are living sacrifices and inspiring examples of sold-out disciples of Jesus. I am so happy to be able to share their hearts with all who read this book.

## Get Out of Here!

One of the single most popular practices was a change in environment. I know. I know. I live in South Florida: God must know how uniquely weak I am and has therefore given me a particularly beautiful place to live in. It is hard not to find a beautiful representation of God's creation here. But wherever you live, God's creation is "find-able." For example, I remember living in Mexico City in 1987 as a young man who was born and raised in a town of 5,000 on the coast of Massachusetts. Suddenly, I found myself in a monstrous city of more than twenty million people and their accompanying buildings, cars and pollution. I would literally go lie on the roof and look up in such a way as to only see the sky, on the days when I needed it most. There was something so refreshing about erasing from view all the monuments to man and technology and looking up into a sky that spoke only of God.

Sometimes the first step in restoring our hearts is to simply get out of the house and get into the woods, walk on the beach, visit the mountains. Don't have any? Find a tree and sit under it. A leaf, an insect, a baby, a sunrise, a sunset or a thunderstorm can be inspirational. Remember:

> When I consider your heavens,
>     the work of your fingers,
> the moon and the stars,
>     which you have set in place,
> what is man that you are mindful of him,
>     the son of man that you care for him? (Psalm 8:3–4)

> In the beginning you laid the foundations of the earth,
>     and the heavens are the work of your hands.
> (Psalm 102:25)

> For since the creation of the world God's invisible quali-
> ties—his eternal power and divine nature—have been

> clearly seen, being understood from what has been
> made, so that men are without excuse. (Romans 1:20)

Why go outside? For some of the members of our staff, it is the quietness that allows them to meditate more deeply, thus taking things deeper into their hearts. I believe there was a reason Jesus found a solitary place in the dark where he could pray (Mark 1:35). Those of us with kids know how important it is to try to get up earlier than they do in the morning. In our house, if you are going to have some deep and quiet time with God, the earlier the better—it gets pretty loud pretty quick.

For others, nature is full of inspiration. A sunrise or a sunset does something to us; it fills us with an awe and respect for the Creator that is hard to come by inside four walls. To the men and women of long ago, each sunrise occurred, not because they understood the rotation of the earth, but because God was faithful and allowed them to see another day.

In addition, nature provides us with a unique place to go and "meet with" God. If I set a place for God in the local restaurant and have a conversation with him during dinner, people are going to imagine the worst about me. Outdoors, I can go for a walk and talk to and feel near him. I can sit on a wall or under a tree and be with him, with so much more freedom than when I am somewhere inside.

## Turn Back the Clock

For many disciples on our staff, softness of heart is just a memory away. Much like the sentiments expressed in chapter 3, "The Height," there is no disputing how good God was to us at our conversion. When they find themselves getting swamped by the pressures of today and the uncertainty of tomorrow, many of our staff members choose to remember the moment of their salvation.

One of my favorite scriptures over the years has been Philippians 1:6 where Paul encourages the disciples with this truth: "being confident of this, that he who began a good work in you will carry it on to completion until the day of Christ Jesus." I have drawn so much strength of heart over the years by reminding myself of God's willingness to save me when I was least "save-able" and by the impossibility that God would begin something in me only to discard it after so much investment.

For some of the staff, remembering their conversions takes them back more than twenty years. No matter the distance, this is one journey we should never grow tired of making. Is there anything that happens to us between our baptism and heaven that should tarnish the memory of our salvation? I think not. I know that we are tempted to forget it all the time, getting bogged down in performance and our own frailty, but we are saved. It really did happen. It really does outweigh all the other experiences we have had or will have on this earth.

Have you forgotten what you have been forgiven of? I frequently rewrite the sins I was forgiven of at my baptism. It is important to me to remember the names of the people I sinned against, not as an exercise in guilt but as a reminder of who I was and am without the help of God. I also believe it is important to understand that the sins I committed prior to my baptism at twenty-one years old were not the "limit" of what I am capable of. They were simply the limit of what I was able to do. Were I to have remained without God, I would have crossed countless new lines and multiplied my sin in both gravity and excess. However, I do not have to look all the way back to my baptism to find grievous sin. Part of softening my heart is to look in the Word at the same lists of sins that convicted me years ago, realizing how many of them still win the battle currently. I have overcome many of the most carnal ones, but I still commit plenty on a daily basis that would make God just in condemning me, were the blood of Christ not available to cleanse me.

Some of the members of the staff still have the Bible and the notes they took in their Bible studies when they became Christians. For them, these things help them remember their state of heart during the most grateful time in their lives. Others go back and visit the shore on which they were baptized or simply call one of the friends who helped them become Christians. One of our staff couples is in the process of adopting their first child. All the work and emotion they are putting into this is a constant reminder of all the work and emotion that God put into their adoptions as his son and daughter.

## A Secret Scriptural Weapon

For many of the members of the staff, there is a certain scripture that seems to always have the power to cut through whatever emotion or situation has them handcuffed. Even though all Scripture is God-breathed and useful, there is a verse or an experience with the Word that reaches them every time.

For many, it is the message of the cross. There is not enough room in this book to detail all the ways in which God's love can reach us through the cross, but there is one thing the staff expressed in common: you have to work at understanding the cross. Insights of yesterday about Jesus' death need to be consistently refreshed. To many of us, Jesus' death on the cross is the single event in the Word that our enemy, Satan, tries to distort or blind us to the most. If he can reduce the value of the cross, make it common or cheap, then what will be left to move us? God has never spoken louder than he did on Calvary. We must constantly let the cross become more and more of what moves us on the deepest level.

More than a few of us live in the Psalms. What a unique gift they are in the Scriptures! Where else can we see so much sustained emotion and passion for God? In the Psalms, David and others work through their emotions in front of our very eyes. We hear and identify with the starting point, and we can learn how they made it to the finish with the convictions they do. There are many of the ministry leaders who wonder aloud whether they could survive without the guide of the Psalms to assure them that it is okay to bring their hearts to God in whatever state and he can and will listen and help.

Quite a few of us like memorizing scriptures and writing them on index cards and carrying them with us. A great exercise is to take a scripture and simply stress a different word every time you recite it. This provides a much richer understanding than we would get by simply passing over the verse once. Look at the following scripture—my personal favorite in all the Bible, Ephesians 3:20—and see how much new meaning you can get from accenting a different word each time you read it.

> "Now to him who is **able** to do immeasurably more than all we ask or imagine, according to his power that is at work within us…"

"Now to him who is able to **do** immeasurably more than all we ask or imagine, according to his power that is at work within us…"

"Now to him who is able to do **immeasurably** more than all we ask or imagine, according to his power that is at work within us…"

"Now to him who is able to do immeasurably **more** than all we ask or imagine, according to his power that is at work within us…"

"Now to him who is able to do immeasurably more than **all** we ask or imagine, according to his power that is at work within us…"

"Now to him who is able to do immeasurably more than all **we** ask or imagine, according to his power that is at work within us…"

"Now to him who is able to do immeasurably more than all we **ask** or imagine, according to his power that is at work within us…"

"Now to him who is able to do immeasurably more than all we ask or **imagine**, according to his power that is at work within us…"

"Now to him who is able to do immeasurably more than all we ask or imagine, according to **his power** that is at work within us…"

"Now to him who is able to do immeasurably more than all we ask or imagine, according to his power that **is at work** within us…"

"Now to him who is able to do immeasurably more than all we ask or imagine, according to his power that is at work **within** us…"

"Now to him who is able to do immeasurably more than all we ask or imagine, according to his power that is at work within **us**…"

See what happens? It is amazing!

## The Best for Last

I guess that the "best" practical suggestion is the one that works for you. Regardless, there were two suggestions that quieted the room. The customary "Amen" that the other suggestions had gotten were changed to "O-o-o-o-oh" upon their revelation. Both were very similar in emphasis and heart, and both will require some real dedication to implement.

One brother has a treasure chest. In his treasure chest, he has placed all the items of most significance in his Christian life:

- His baptism photos and those of the men he has baptized are there.
- Extra-special notes and letters from his dearest friends are there.
- His wedding vows are inside.
- Memorabilia from the birth of his son is safely tucked there.
- And so much more…

How could you not get sensitized to God and his blessings by looking through that!

One sister has a scrapbook, which is similar, but unique. Her scrapbook is all about the heart of God. She has gone through magazines, photos and all kinds of other resources to create a testament to the heart of God. His qualities, sentiments and convictions are represented on every page and added to frequently. What an encouragement! Can you imagine anything more encouraging than to flip through an entire scrapbook devoted to representing the heart of God?

This is by no means a definitive list of all that can be done practically to help our hearts. Our prayer as the South Florida Church staff is that we can inspire you with this little list and that you will come up with your own and *pass it around*. It will all come back our way as we "encourage each other with these words" (1 Thessalonians 4:18).

# 12

# FOREVER SEEKING

What have we thought in the past about falling in love with God? Maybe that it will happen on a couple of minutes a day or that it will happen by bringing the same old things to him in prayer. Sometimes falling in love with God again remains elusive for a long time, and people forget that it is attainable. The truth is, we find what we seek.

- If we seek for relief in the act of salvation, this is what we find.
- If we seek acceptance and a community, this is what we find.
- If we seek wisdom and insight, then this is what we find.
- If we seek an effective ministry, then this is what we find.
- If we seek to love God more and more deeply, we will find it.

What are you seeking?

> "And you, my son Solomon, acknowledge the God of your father, and serve him with wholehearted devotion and with a willing mind, for the LORD searches every heart and understands every motive behind the thoughts. If you seek him, he will be found by you; but if you forsake him, he will reject you forever. Consider now, for the LORD has chosen you to build a temple as a sanctuary. Be strong and do the work." (1 Chronicles 28:9–10)

"Be strong and do the work," but first *seek* him. How many times have I felt the exhaustion of trying to do the work without seeking him first? When I share my faith with people, am I really sharing with them the joy of seeking or the commitment to work? When I talk about my church, what do I find praiseworthy? That we are committed to a mission or committed to seeking our God? How can I do his work without seeking his help, his wisdom and his direction?

Does God really just toss his people out into the harvest field of the world and expect them to work *only?* Is his communication limited to directives about the work of helping others? Does he not want to give his Holy Spirit to comfort, encourage, convict? Does he not want to share in the victories so "that the sower and the reaper can be glad together?" (John 4:36). At some point we will all learn that none of us can "be strong" without seeking. Talent, experience and insight are cheap gifts and can never take the place of a heart that genuinely seeks God.

If you have read this book at a pace of one chapter a day, then only twelve days have elapsed on this leg of your journey. To get some perspective on this, imagine the following: if you became a Christian in your twenties, your journey with God will last for an average of almost 15,000 days. It is good to have a dozen refreshing days in a row, but it is barely a step or two toward the finish line in the entire journey. For these twelve chapters to have a marked effect on your life, it will be necessary to create a habit of seeking. There are many decisions that you need to make with regard to your relationship with God.

- How much time should go by without a special prayer time?

- How many times a month or year should I spend the entire evening in prayer?
- How often should I get away from all the pressures of my "daily life" so that I can experience the profound quiet and intense communion of uninterrupted seeking?
- What am I trying to accomplish in my Bible study?
- What do I need to do to allow the message of God to really soak into my heart?
- Who can I learn from around me who obviously abides in God more passionately than I?
- When do I get the extra time with God that my heart keeps telling me I need?
- Where can I go and be really free to wrestle emotionally with the will of God?

When Solomon had finished the temple of the LORD and the royal palace, and had succeeded in carrying out all he had in mind to do in the temple of the LORD and in his own palace, the LORD appeared to him at night and said:

"I have heard your prayer and have chosen this place for myself as a temple for sacrifices.

"When I shut up the heavens so that there is no rain, or command locusts to devour the land or send a plague among my people, if my people, who are called by my name, will humble themselves and pray and seek my face and turn from their wicked ways, then will I hear from heaven and will forgive their sin and will heal their land. Now my eyes will be open and my ears attentive to the prayers offered in this place. I have chosen and consecrated this temple so that my Name may be there forever. My eyes and my heart will always be there." (2 Chronicles 7:11–16)

Even after the temple is built, God is concerned with whether his people will still seek him. A. W. Tozer's great concern, which prompted his writing of *The Pursuit of God*, was that God himself was so often "felt" but not "found" by people. God does so much to be felt by us, intervening constantly in this world and in our lives. The difference between felt and found, however, is whether or not we decide to seek him. For example, our church in South Florida is "large" by most standards, with more than 3,000 in attendance each Sunday. I am sure that people feel God at different times and in different ways each week as a result of being members. This is wonderful, but of little lasting value unless that experience prompts people to seek him in a deeply personal and individual manner. I am sure that God has the same concern today that he did in Solomon's time—will people still seek him?—especially when the structure around them seems "complete."

David clearly understood the imperative of seeking the Lord.

> Why, O Lord, do you stand far off?
>> Why do you hide yourself in times of trouble?
> In his arrogance the wicked man hunts down the weak,
>> who are caught in the schemes he devises.
> He boasts of the cravings of his heart;
>> he blesses the greedy and reviles the Lord.
> *In his pride the wicked does not seek him;*
>> in all his thoughts there is no room for God.
> (Psalm 10:1–4, emphasis mine)

> The earth is the Lord's, and everything in it,
>> the world, and all who live in it;

for he founded it upon the seas
    and established it upon the waters.
Who may ascend the hill of the Lord?
    Who may stand in his holy place?
He who has clean hands and a pure heart,
    who does not lift up his soul to an idol
    or swear by what is false.
He will receive blessing from the Lord
    and vindication from God his Savior.
*Such is the generation of those who seek him,*
    *who seek your face, O God of Jacob.*
(Psalm 24:1–6, emphasis mine)

The Lord is my light and my salvation—
    whom shall I fear?
The Lord is the stronghold of my life—
    of whom shall I be afraid?
When evil men advance against me
    to devour my flesh,
when my enemies and my foes attack me,
    they will stumble and fall.
Though an army besiege me,
    my heart will not fear;
though war break out against me,
    even then will I be confident.
*One thing I ask of the Lord,*
    *this is what I seek:*
*that I may dwell in the house of the Lord*
    *all the days of my life,*
*to gaze upon the beauty of the Lord*
    *and to seek him in his temple.*
For in the day of trouble

he will keep me safe in his dwelling;
he will hide me in the shelter of his tabernacle
    and set me high upon a rock.
Then my head will be exalted
    above the enemies who surround me;
at his tabernacle will I sacrifice with shouts of joy;
    I will sing and make music to the LORD.
Hear my voice when I call, O LORD;
    be merciful to me and answer me.
*My heart says of you, "Seek his face!"*
    *Your face, LORD, I will seek.*
Do not hide your face from me,
    do not turn your servant away in anger;
    you have been my helper.
Do not reject me or forsake me,
    O God my Savior. (Psalm 27:1–9)

Perhaps in the journey through this book you have been helped by God to clarify what you have been seeking. I know of many times in my life when I sought a blessing more than God himself. Vindication, relief and answers have many times been the object of my journey, instead of the face of God. God has doggedly frustrated my quest on more than one occasion in order to purify my motives. Nothing will satisfy like seeking his face. How long does vindication last? How far can I ride the wave of relief in a given situation? For how many days do I feel satisfied by an answer—no matter how complex the question? David found his delight in heeding the call of his heart to seek God's face and "seek him in his temple."

So, when does seeking really start? For many of us, we would like to think that we were seeking God as an antecedent to studying the Bible. It is noble and romantic to imagine ourselves pining away for God on our bed of suffering before someone heeded our heart's desire and invited us to church or we stumble upon the kingdom "ourselves." The only problem with this is the truth in the Scriptures! And this is quite a problem. In Romans 3:11, Paul seems to be stating a spiritual principle when he writes that it is written that there is "no one who seeks God." Can we bear that the impetus behind us becoming Christians does not start with us? Can we accept that, as Jesus stated, "No one can come to me unless the Father who sent me draws him"? (John 6:44).

We start off on the wrong foot when we imagine that our seeking begins our walk with God. It is actually his seeking us that orchestrates the elements. His work in our life always precedes our prayers to be saved. I am sure that other people's prayers for me—in particular, my sister's—were the catalyst that started the dominoes falling in my life, more than any seeking of my own. What happens when we start studying the Bible is simply that we allow ourselves to be sought by God. We become open to the Seeker of our souls, and we begin to learn about the One who loves enough to go to any length and pay any price for our redemption. Too many times I would look back on my own conversion in the following way:

1. I was seeking God.
2. I got invited to church by a Christian.
3. Since I was seeking, I was open to studying the Bible.
4. In the studies to become a Christian, I found God.
5. I got baptized and began my Christian life.

Not only does this fundamentally reassign who gets the credit for my salvation (me because I was seeking God, instead of God because he sought me and drew me to him), but also this makes my baptism seem like the end of the quest! How ridiculous is this? Can I really be saying that the nine days I studied the Bible to become a Christian were enough to grasp the magnitude of God himself so that I could smugly end the journey at the waters of baptism? There is simply no way. The great men and women of faith spent their entire lives "seeking." Can you imagine how the apostle Paul or King David would react to our attitude of "I found him; I am saved; there is not much more to do now"? I think they would tell us that we are missing out on the greatest adventure of all time: the journey. There is very little falling out of love, getting bored and burdened, and feeling disillusioned in our relationship with God unless we think we have already found him.

## Active Learners

To continually seek him means a commitment to "active learning." As I write this, my ankle is in a cast. I got it stepped on as I tried to run in a 5K race in downtown Miami last week. The doctor told me that "at my age" it is better for me to break my ankle than to sprain it as I did. This is the first of plenty "at your age" comments I am sure to hear. At some point I will have to accept that certain sports and athletic pursuits are so much more difficult the older I get. I wince each year as we begin a church flag-football league, wondering which of my like-aged friends is going to be forced into realizing through injury that the "glory days" of physical prowess are long gone. I am more limited the older I get, and I have to accept this. I will not die when I lose my competitive edge on a playing field. However, we all "die" when we stop learning.

My father is seventy-three years young and is as avid a learner as he ever was. He has published three books since "retiring" (a flexible term in his vocabulary). I am so proud to get the clippings in the mail from our hometown newspaper that show him signing books at Barnes & Noble or lecturing to elementary students about the maritime history around Cape Cod. He took up computing in his late sixties, Web design a few years later and electronic publishing after that. He is proof positive that we never have to stop learning. Our minds can constantly enlarge and grasp new concepts. There is no time limit this side of death. Anyone can learn. We all learn at different paces and in different situations. What teaches one is lost on another—until a different time in life when the latter learns what he could have earlier. Learning is one of those magical elements God allows us to experience in this life, like love, compassion and happiness, that is a masterpiece of heavenly participation.

When we are young, we do not grasp learning right away. We understand obligation ("I gotta go to school"). At this point in our lives, we are forced into learning, and we usually have a preformed opinion about it from someone older than we are ("It's boring!" "It's exciting!" "You gotta go or you'll be a loser!"). No matter what the initial impression is, at some point "it" happens: someone reaches us and opens up our minds to the possibilities of learning. How exciting! How formative! We get handed a key and start unlocking doors to history, to this world and even to our own minds. We develop a curiosity and an appetite for something. It starts small—it could be a certain animal, a sport, a character in a book—but it captures us and we are off. This is where these incredible people called "teachers" come into play. They are the ones who activate our minds; the good ones connect with and change people.

And then something completely crazy happens: we graduate from high school, we may go to college and choose a major, or we start to work and have something we focus on…and so we narrow our desire to learn. It all becomes about a specialty—nursing or mechanics or accounting or raising kids—and we stop being hungry to learn. We become "passive learners."

Because we are busy or our environment gets much more predictable, we may keep closing ourselves off to experiences and opportunities to learn more. We merely want to learn what we need to know to get a good grade, a promotion, or simply to have survival skills. We graduate into our life and we start stagnating mentally, intellectually, emotionally. The high notes get all muted, the inspiration (and there may be nothing more important than this) disappears, and we become a collection of crystallized thoughts. The people around us even know what we are going to say in any given situation. We become intellectual statues, frozen in the position we were in the last time we really learned something.

What happened to our ability to learn? Did it die? No, we have just become too passive. For example:

- *We listen to the voice of our experience as the final authority.* We become our own teacher, coach, director—never mind that we are incapable of objective thought about ourselves (Jeremiah 17:9), never mind our ability to deceive ourselves (1 John 1:8).

- *We "learn" mostly from our mistakes.* Usually this means vowing, "I will never do that again"—after the fact. Although better than not learning from mistakes, it is such a minimal exposure to learning. And how often does this kind of learning occur? It depends on how much we mess up!

- *We relinquish the control in our lives over the learning process.* We "learn" from crises, catastrophes, illnesses, deaths, love or friendship, but most of these opportunities merely happen to us. Therefore, we have gone through grammar school, middle school, high school, college, and even graduate school by logging many hours of reading, practicing, reciting, writing, memorizing, rehearsing, experimenting and producing to leave it all behind and just let life "happen" to us?

The same learning pattern happens in the in the church. When we initially study the Bible, we have such an incredible, eye-opening, heart-opening time! Remember when you really looked into the Word for the first time? I could not believe how specific, clear, visionary and universal it was! Then, as a young Christian, we may get a hold of some follow-up studies, but most people are already in a decline after their baptism! We stop *learning* and focus on maintenance. We study out topics like: What do I need to do to become a _____? How should I raise my kids so that they do what is right? What do I need to study to overcome the sin of _____?

Have you ever thought about how arrogant this posture is? There are sixty-six books of the Bible, written over a period of many, many centuries. Thousands upon thousands of teachings, insights, warnings and heartfelt counsel reveal God's heart and love for us. And we are going to say "I got it" after a couple of weeks? In this case, we need to ask ourselves if we really became Christians to have a relationship with God, or did we just want something from him—like salvation, peace, fellowship or a better marriage? The treasures are for those who will continue to seek forever, not for those who want tips and tricks on being "effective," whatever that might mean.

I see how I have taught people to be satisfied with so little. When I am not personally and actively seeking to learn from God, I am teaching others to be content with a little understanding or an occasional insight. In my zeal to have an answer for someone, I am stealing from them the opportunity to learn from the Lord themselves. If people come first to me for counsel and help, then I am teaching them to be dependent on man (who will ultimately disappoint) instead of God, in whom all the riches of knowledge and understanding reside.

I have seen many who have not been active learners for so long that they have forgotten more verses than they have learned! God created us to all be active learners and active seekers. Here's a great example from the lives of Jesus and the apostles:

> One day Jesus was praying in a certain place. When he finished, one of his disciples said to him, "Lord, teach us to pray, just as John taught his disciples."
> He said to them, "When you pray, say:
>> "'Father,
>> hallowed be your name,
>> your kingdom come.
>> Give us each day our daily bread.
>> Forgive us our sins,
>>> for we also forgive everyone who sins
>>> against us.
>> And lead us not into temptation.'"

Then he said to them, "Suppose one of you has a friend, and he goes to him at midnight and says, 'Friend, lend me three loaves of bread, because a friend of mine on a journey has come to me, and I have nothing to set before him.'

"Then the one inside answers, 'Don't bother me. The door is already locked, and my children are with me in bed. I can't get up and give you anything.' I tell you, though he will not get up and give him the bread because he is his friend, yet because of the man's boldness he will get up and give him as much as he needs.

"So I say to you: Ask and it will be given to you; seek and you will find; knock and the door will be opened to you. For everyone who asks receives; he who seeks finds; and to him who knocks, the door will be opened.

"Which of you fathers, if your son asks for a fish, will give him a snake instead? Or if he asks for an egg, will give him a scorpion? If you then, though you are evil, know how to give good gifts to your children, how much more will your Father in heaven give the Holy Spirit to those who ask him!" (Luke 11:1–13)

Let's think through this for a minute. Aren't these grown men? Aren't these men who already had professions? Haven't these men already learned great spiritual truths from John the Baptist? But they have a hunger. Now, think about this: if there were ever a moment to be a passive learner, it would be when you walk with Jesus. I mean, he probably has a plan, right? So why did they ask their own questions? Why not just follow the syllabus?

Where would the disciples have been had they not decided to be active learners? According to this passage, they might not have learned that God could be addressed as Father! This would not be something to miss. They learned this life-changing truth because they chose to be active, not passive. They took the responsibility upon themselves to get deep and ask questions— when it would have been more comfortable to sit back and be guided. They took advantage of a chance to learn despite their age, background or prior perfection. They were *actively* seeking. They asked questions of their teacher and Lord, and they were hardly disappointed. They learned because they first decided to seek. No matter how great a teacher you have, knowledge and wisdom is hidden if you have not first made this decision to seek.

I wish you all the best on your journey. I pray that this book has encouraged you to draw near to our Father with more confidence and expectation. Remember:

> "No eye has seen,
>     no ear has heard,
> no mind has conceived
>     what God has prepared for those who love him."
> (1 Corinthians 2:9)

# WHO ARE WE?

Discipleship Publications International (DPI) began publishing in 1993. We are a nonprofit Christian publisher affiliated with the International Churches of Christ, committed to publishing and distributing materials that honor God, lift up Jesus Christ and show how his message practically applies to all areas of life. We have a deep conviction that no one changes life like Jesus and that the implementation of his teaching will revolutionize any life, any marriage, any family and any singles household.

Since our beginning, we have published more than 110 titles; plus, we have produced a number of important, spiritual audio products. More than one million volumes have been printed, and our works have been translated into more than a dozen languages—international is not just a part of our name! Our books are shipped regularly to every inhabited continent.

To see a more detailed description of our works, find us on the World Wide Web at www.dpibooks.org. You can order books by calling 1-888-DPI-BOOK twenty-four hours a day. From outside the US, call 978-670-8840 during Boston-area business hours.

We appreciate the hundreds of comments we have received from readers. We would love to hear from you. Here are other ways to get in touch:

**Mail:** DPI, 2 Sterling Road, Billerica, Mass. 01862-2595
**E-Mail:** dpibooks@icoc.org

# FIND US ON THE WORLD WIDE WEB

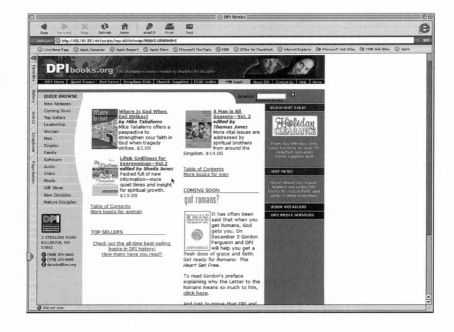

www.dpibooks.org

1-888-DPI-BOOK

Outside the US, call

978-670-8840